AS/A-LEVEL YEAR 1

STUDENT GUIDE

EDEXCEL

Politics

UK government

Neil McNaughton

Series editor: Eric Magee

HODDER
EDUCATION
AN HACHETTE UK COMPANY

Hodder Education, an Hachette UK company, Blenheim Court, George Street, Banbury, Oxfordshire OX16 5BH

Orders

Bookpoint Ltd, 130 Park Drive, Milton Park, Abingdon, Oxfordshire OX14 4SB

tel: 01235 827827

fax: 01235 400401

e-mail: education@bookpoint.co.uk

Lines are open 9.00 a.m.–5.00 p.m., Monday to Saturday, with a 24-hour message answering service. You can also order through the Hodder Education website: www.hoddereducation.co.uk

© Neil McNaughton 2017

ISBN 978-1-4718-9290-5

First printed 2017

Impression number 5 4 3 2 1

Year 2021 2020 2019 2018 2017

This Guide has been written specifically to support students preparing for the Edexcel AS and A-level Politics examinations. The content has been neither approved nor endorsed by Edexcel and remains the sole responsibility of the author.

Typeset by Integra Software Services Pvt. Ltd., Pondicherry, India

Printed in Italy

Hachette UK's policy is to use papers that are natural, renewable and recyclable products and made from wood grown in sustainable forests. The logging and manufacturing processes are expected to conform to the environmental regulations of the country of origin.

Contents

Content Guidance

Questions & Answers

AS-style questions

A-level-style questions

■ Getting the most from this book

Questions & Answers

understanding of the significance of the constitution being uncodified, the subject of the question.

⊜ AO1: 5/5 marks, AO2: 5/5 marks

For examples of 30-mark questions see A-level exemplars. Note that 30-mark questions for AS will always begin with a brief quotation and the words: 'How far do you agree…', while A-level 30-mark questions always begin with the command 'Evaluate…'. However, the content of, and approach to, both kinds of question are essentially similar, although the A-level questions also require relevant knowledge and understanding of UK politics and core political ideas.

Parliament
Question 1
Describe the role and importance of departmental select committees.   [10 marks]

⊜ Clearly the answer must explain what the departmental select committees are and what their powers and main features are. Prominent examples of the committees should be described. The main part of the answer should explain their significance. In doing so, some examples of their work should be included. At least two examples would be ideal.

Student answer

The departmental select committees were set up in 1979 to address the problem that Parliament was unable to call government to account effectively enough. Before the committees there was only question time for ministers and this was not working. There are usually 11 members of the committees. In recent years the memberships have been elected by backbench MPs and the chairs are also elected and receive an additional salary. Although the government has a majority on each committee it is expected that the members act in an independent way and often their reports and recommendations will be unanimous. Some of the chairs are also members of the opposition party. ⊠

They have the role of examining the work of a government department. They have the power to call witnesses including ministers, civil servants and advisers and may also examine outside experts and other witnesses. They are concerned about how effectively the department works, they look at how efficient they are and whether their policies are fair and take minorities into account. Sometimes they may be critical because of undue delay. Their style is like that of a court of law and witnesses are often cross-examined quite severely. At the end of an investigation they produce a report to the rest of Parliament. The reports are often highly critical and recommend changes to policy. Ministers and civil servants worry about appearing before them because they may be given a tough time. ⊠

Select committees have produced important reports in the past over the behaviour of the press in the phone hacking scandal which led to the Leveson inquiry, over the supply of equipment to UK troops in Afghanistan and Iraq and over the poor performance of the NHS, especially A & E and over problems in

58 Edexcel Politics

Commentary on sample student answers

Read the comments (preceded by the icon ⊜) showing how many marks each answer would be awarded in the exam and exactly where marks are gained or lost.

Exam-style questions

Commentary on the questions

Tips on what you need to do to gain full marks, indicated by the icon ⊜

Sample student answers

Practise the questions, then look at the student answers that follow.

■ About this book

The aim of this Student Guide is to prepare you for the Edexcel AS and A-level Paper 2 UK Government (excluding Non-core Political Ideas) examinations. Paper 2 is worth 50% of the Politics AS and a third of the Politics A-level, and all of the topics covered in this guide could be examined in the exam. It is therefore vital that you are familiar and confident with all the material.

The **Content Guidance** section covers all the topics largely in the order that they appear on the Edexcel A-level specification, UK Government section. You are strongly advised to have a copy of the most recent version of the specification to refer to as you go through the topics. There are four main topics:

- The constitution
- Parliament
- Prime minister and executive
- Relationships between the branches

Each of these sections is further divided into three subsections.

You should use the Content Guidance to ensure you are familiar with all the key concepts and terms, statistics, issues and arguments, and have a range of relevant examples you can quote in your answers to show you are aware of the relative significance of these principles and concepts.

The **Questions & Answers** section provides an opportunity to hone your exam technique and to become familiar with the skills and structures that examiners are looking for. The answers illustrate both good and weak technique. It is not possible to provide sample questions and answers for each section of the exam on every topic, so you need to be aware that any parts of the specification could be tested in any sections of the examination.

This guide does not provide a complete range of examples or go into full detail, so you should use it alongside other resources such as class notes, the *Edexcel AS/A-level UK Government and Politics* textbook by Neil McNaughton (ISBN 978-1-4718-8931-8) and articles in *Politics Review* (both published by Hodder Education). You should also use websites such as the BBC, TotalPolitics.com, The Times Red Box and www.politics.co.uk to keep up to date with current news.

Content Guidance

■ The constitution

Before looking specifically at the UK Constitution, you should know what a constitution — the constitution of *any* country — actually does and why it exists. A constitution has the following key functions:

- It distributes power between political institutions, both between the centre and regions, and between institutions at the centre.
- It establishes how institutions relate to each other.
- It usually specifies the main processes of government such as the electoral system and the legislative process.
- It normally specifies the limits to government overall.
- It establishes the civil rights and freedoms of the citizens.
- It establishes who is a citizen and how one can become a citizen.
- It establishes the method by which the constitution can be amended.

The UK Constitution is very different in nature to most constitutions in democratic countries, but it still performs the functions described above.

The nature and sources of the UK Constitution

The UK Constitution is unique in the democratic world. Here we look at the ways in which it has developed, its unique characteristics and the sources of the constitution which come to us from a variety of origins.

The development of the UK Constitution

Most democratic countries' constitutions are created at one moment in history. This did not happen in the UK. Instead the constitution has evolved through a number of important historical and legislative occurrences. Table 1 traces the stages in its development.

Rule of law The democratic principle that everyone, including government itself, should be subject equally to the law.

Parliamentary sovereignty The key principle of the UK Constitution which establishes that the Westminster Parliament has supreme power. It is the source of all political power and is omnicompetent, meaning it can pass any law it chooses.

Table 1 The historical development of the UK Constitution

Date	Development	Nature of change
1215	Magna Carta	Mostly now out of date, but this established the principle of the **rule of law**.
1688–89	The Glorious Revolution and Bill of Rights	King James II was deposed and replaced by William III. The Bill of Rights established the **sovereignty of Parliament** and its supremacy over the monarch.
1701	Act of Settlement	Among other terms, this Act established the monarch as ruler of the whole of the United Kingdom.
1911 and 1949	Parliament Acts	Limited the power of the House of Lords and so established the House of Commons as superior to the Lords.
1972	European Communities Act	Brought the UK into the European Union; since rescinded.

Date	Development	Nature of change
1998	Devolution Acts	Large amounts of power were transferred from Westminster to governments in Wales, Scotland and Northern Ireland.
1998	Human Rights Act	Brought the European Convention on Human Rights into UK law.
2005	Constitutional Reform Act	The Supreme Court was established, thus confirming the independence of the judiciary.
2017	The UK agrees to leave the EU	Following a referendum in 2016, the UK began the process of leaving the EU and so repatriating all national sovereignty.

The nature of the UK Constitution

So far this is a little confusing. We know how the UK Constitution developed but we do not know where to find it and we do not know what its main characteristics are. It is therefore necessary to establish the nature of the constitution. The main features are these:

- **It is uncodified.** This means it is not written down in one single place, nor can it be found in any organised form.
- **It is not entrenched**. This means there is nothing to protect it from being changed by a simple process, normally an Act of Parliament. **Entrenchment** implies safeguards to prevent the constitution being amended too easily and without evidence of widespread consent.
- **It has a variety of sources**. This means it can be found in several forms and in a large number of separate documents and principles.
- **It is unitary**. In a unitary constitution sovereignty, or ultimate power, lies in one place. In the UK this is the Westminster Parliament. In non-unitary, **federal constitutions** (such as the USA) sovereignty is divided both within central institutions and between the centre and the regions.
- **It is not supreme**. Constitutional laws look exactly the same as ordinary laws and are created — by Parliament — in the same way. Furthermore, Parliament in the UK is sovereign and so can change the constitution at will. In other words, Parliament stands above the constitution. This is not the case in most democratic countries.
- **It is very flexible**. Because it is not entrenched and because it is under the control of Parliament the UK Constitution can be changed very easily, by simple Act of Parliament. All that is required is that a majority of members of Parliament will back an amendment or new element.

Exam tip

Many exam questions refer to the uncodified nature of the UK Constitution. You should remember that it is just as important that the constitution is unentrenched. Indeed, the principle of codification also implies entrenchment, so treat the two principles as one.

The main sources of the UK Constitution

When we speak of a 'source' of the constitution, what we really mean is the various elements that make up the constitution. As we have seen, in most democratic states,

Knowledge check 1

Look at Table 1 and answer these questions:

a Which developments established key constitutional principles?
b Which developments marked significant transfers of power from some institutions to others?
c Which developments specifically affected the distribution of sovereignty?

Entrenchment
A constitutional principle whereby constitutional rules are safeguarded against change by a future government or legislature.

Federal constitution
A federal constitution, such as those operating in the USA and Germany, is one where ultimate power — sovereignty — is divided between central government and regional governments.

the constitution is found in a single legal document. This is not the case in the UK. Table 2 shows the different sources of the UK Constitution.

Table 2 Sources of the UK Constitution

Type of source	Description	Examples
Parliamentary statutes	An Act of Parliament, passed in the same way as any other Acts	The Human Rights Act 1998 (see Table 1) The Parliament Acts 1911 and 1949 (see Table 1)
Constitutional conventions	Unwritten principles that are accepted as binding within the political community	The Salisbury Convention that the House of Lords must not obstruct proposals contained in the governing party's last election manifesto The recent convention that important constitutional changes need the approval of a referendum
Established principles	Principles that are binding because they have existed over a long period	The sovereignty of Parliament has existed since 1689 The rule of law has arguably existed since Magna Carta in 1215 The royal prerogative is a key principle (see a longer description below)
Common law	Unwritten laws established through the courts over a long period of time	Many of the rights of citizens exist though common law, maintained by the judges
Historical documents (authoritative works)	These are great works of legal authority which act as guides to the operation of the constitution.	Blackstone's *Commentaries* of 1765 clearly defined parliamentary sovereignty Bagehot's *English Constitution* of 1867 defined the role of the cabinet and its relationship with Parliament

Key principles of the constitution

These are therefore the key principles or features of the UK Constitution:

1 **Parliamentary sovereignty.** Parliament is legally and politically supreme.

2 **The royal prerogative.** Prerogative powers refer to those powers which were once in the hands of the monarch. They could be exercised without the need to seek parliamentary approval. Over several centuries these powers have been transferred to the prime minister (PM) and his or her government. The powers involved are:

- commander-in-chief of the armed forces
- foreign policy maker
- negotiating foreign treaties
- control of cabinet
- the appointment and dismissal of government ministers
- the granting of honours including peerages and knighthoods

3 **The independence of the judiciary.** The judges who administer justice, interpret the law and the constitution and protect citizens' rights are independent of political pressure.

4 **The rule of law.** All citizens and government itself are equal under the law.

5 **The fusion of powers.** The executive (government) and the legislature (Parliament) are not separated in the UK. This means that members of the government are also Members of Parliament, in other words, the government is drawn from Parliament, and this implies that the

Constitutional convention An unwritten rule of the constitution which everyone in the political community accepts as binding. New conventions are constantly developing.

government is able to dominate Parliament. The opposite of this is the *separation of powers*, which is absent in the UK.

6 **Executive dominance.** This is a political principle which is so important it can be described as constitutional. It means that the executive branch dominates the legislature. Parliamentary sovereignty does mean that Parliament can defy government, but it rarely does.

7 **Responsible government.** It is a firm principle that all elected bodies, at all levels, must be **accountable**, or responsible, for what they do. They are accountable to the electorate at election time, and to elected representative bodies such as the UK Parliament between elections.

8 **Devolution.** A recent development, this means that power, though not sovereignty, is divided between the centre and the governments of the national regions of Scotland, Wales and Northern Ireland.

How the UK Constitution has changed since 1997

Reform of the UK Constitution, 1997–2010

There was very little constitutional reform in the UK in the hundred years before 1997. The powers of the House of Lords were curtailed under the Parliament Acts of 1911 and 1949, life peerages were introduced in 1958 (before that all peers in the House of Lords were hereditary) and departmental **select committees** were introduced in the House of Commons in 1979. However, these were modest reforms and made no *fundamental* changes to how government and politics worked in the UK.

Real reform began in 1997 with the election of a Labour government under Tony Blair. You should have a thorough knowledge of the following reforms:

- Electoral reform, 1998
- Devolution, 1998
- Human Rights Act 1998
- Reform of the House of Lords, 1999
- Reform of the Supreme Court, 2005

You should also be aware of:

- the Freedom of Information Act 2000
- the introduction of an elected mayor in London, 1998
- the reform of select committees in the House of Commons whereby members and chairs were elected by MPs
- the introduction of a backbench business committee
- the constitutional significance of the UK leaving the EU

Table 3 shows the reasons for the reforms, together with the specific legislation and the nature of the reform.

Accountability The democratic principle that all elected individuals must be accountable to those who have elected them and so can face criticism and may, under extreme circumstances, be removed.

Knowledge check 2

According to the principles and features of the UK political constitution, which bodies have the following responsibilities?

- Making laws
- Appointing members of the cabinet
- Interpreting the meaning of law
- Protecting citizens' rights
- Establishing regional policies

Select committee Despite the name, these are permanent committees of backbenchers who are scrutinising the work of government.

Table 3 Constitutional reforms, 1997–2010 (summarised)

Reform	Year	Legislation	Detail
Devolution	1997/98	Scotland Act Wales Act Northern Ireland Act	The transfer of considerable powers to governments and elected bodies in the three countries
Electoral reform	1998	Scotland Act Wales Act Northern Ireland Act	The devolution settlement, including the introduction of new electoral systems in the three countries: STV (single transferable vote) in Northern Ireland, AMS (additional member system) in Scotland and Wales
Human Rights	1998	Human Rights Act	Brought the European Convention on Human Rights into UK law, making it fully binding
House of Lords reform	1999	House of Lords Act	Most of the hereditary peers were removed, leaving only 92 in the House of Lords. It became a mostly appointed chamber
Supreme Court	2005	Constitutional Reform Act	Twelve of the most senior judges were removed from the House of Lords, forming a fully independent Supreme Court as the highest court in the country

The purposes of the 1997–2010 reforms were as follows:
- To make the UK generally more democratic
- To bring the constitution into line with other modern systems
- To decentralise power away from central government
- To improve the status of human rights in the UK

Reform of the UK Constitution, 2010–15

You should have a thorough knowledge of the main reforms undertaken by the coalition government of 2010–15. These were:
- the Fixed Term Parliaments Act 2011
- further devolution to Wales, 2012

You should also be aware of two more constitutional changes since 2015:
- English votes for English laws, 2015
- the Recall of MPs Act 2015

Reforms of the UK Constitution since 2015

Three main developments have taken place:
- the final decision to leave the European Union in 2016/17
- further devolution to Scotland and Wales
- devolution of powers to city regions

Exam tip

The increasing use of referendums to resolve constitutional issues is not, strictly speaking, a constitutional *reform*, but a constitutional *development*. However, when discussing reforms you should include the *convention* that a referendum is usually needed to approve important constitutional changes.

Knowledge check 3

Looking at the constitutional reforms between 1997 and 2010, identify:
- two reforms that will enhance human rights in the UK
- a reform that has decentralised power
- two reforms that make the UK more democratic

Table 4 Reforms, 2010 to current (summarised)

Reform	Year	Legislation	Detail
Fixed-term parliaments	2011	Fixed Term Parliaments Act	Except under exceptional circumstances, general elections must be held at regular 5-year intervals. This used to be under the control of the prime minister.
Further devolution to Wales	2016	Government of Wales Act	The Welsh government has the power to apply to the UK Parliament for additional powers, including over taxation and law making.
Further devolution to Scotland	2016	Scotland Act	More powers were devolved to Scotland, in particular power over a range of taxes, including income tax, and over some welfare benefits.
Exit from the European Union	2017–19	2016 referendum and European Union (Notification of Withdrawal) Act 2017	The exit from the European Union has wide-ranging constitutional implications.
Devolution to city regions	2017	Various agreements between the UK government and city governments	Elected mayors with considerable powers transferred from Westminster in city regions such as Manchester, Birmingham and Liverpool.

Summary of key reforms

We can now summarise the key reforms which are identified in the specification and explain the main effects of each one.

Devolution

This is the transfer of significant powers, *but not sovereignty*, to regional governments and elected assemblies in Scotland, Wales and Northern Ireland. Each of the three countries have received different types of power but the main policy areas devolved to all three are health, education, transport and social care. Power has been considerably decentralised and democracy is more regionally based. Devolution powers have been extended in Scotland and Wales since 1998.

Electoral reform

Attempts to reform the electoral system for general elections in the UK have all failed. However, the devolved Scottish Parliament and Welsh Assembly are elected by the partly proportional additional member system (AMS), while the Northern Ireland Assembly is elected by single transferable vote (STV). In all three cases the outcome of elections is much more proportionally accurate than is the case at Westminster. Most argue the devolved political systems are more democratic than in Westminster.

Human Rights Act

This Act brought the European Convention on Human Rights into UK law. Everyone in the UK must abide by the convention, although the UK's sovereign parliament can set these rights aside under exceptional circumstances. This was a huge step in extending and protecting rights in the UK.

House of Lords reform

Attempts to introduce an elected second chamber have all failed. The 1999 reform was modest, reducing the number of hereditary peers to just 92. This gave the Lords *slightly* more legitimacy, though it remains unelected and therefore unaccountable.

Knowledge check 4

Looking at the constitutional reforms since 2010, identify:
- three reforms that decentralise power
- one reform that affects sovereignty in the UK
- one reform that affected prime ministerial power

The Supreme Court

The 2005 reform, implemented in 2009, established a fully independent Supreme Court, completely separate from the other branches of government. There is a legal requirement for government to protect its independence. The Supreme Court protects human rights and imposes the rule of law. This significantly improves the protection of rights in the UK and strengthens the ability of judges to check the power of government.

Fixed-term parliaments

Before the 2011 measure, the prime minister could choose the date of a general election. This Act established fixed 5-year terms for each parliament. An early election can only be triggered by a two-thirds majority of the House of Commons, as occurred in 2017 when Theresa May asked for an election on 8 June, or by a vote of no confidence in the House of Commons. This restricted an important prerogative power of the prime minister.

The UK leaves the European Union

This has two major constitutional implications. The first is that the sovereignty transferred to the EU in various treaties has been returned to the UK Parliament. The second is that the European Court of Justice no longer has any jurisdiction in the UK.

Finally, a timeline summarising all constitutional reform since 1997:

1997/98	Devolution of power to Scotland and Wales
1998	Devolution of power to Northern Ireland
1998	Human Rights Act
1998	Registration of Political Parties Act
1999	Greater London Authority Act (elected mayor)
1999	House of Lords Act
2000	Freedom of Information Act
2005	Constitutional Reform Act (Supreme Court)
2006	Government of Wales Act (law-making powers granted)
2010	Elections of House of Commons select committees
2010	Introduction of House of Commons Backbench Business Committee
2011	Fixed Term Parliaments Act
2011	Extension of Welsh law-making powers
2015	Recall of MPs Act
2015	Introduction of English Votes for English Laws (EVEL)
2016	Scotland Act (extends Scottish devolution)
2016	The UK votes to leave the European Union
2017	Elected mayors introduced in Manchester, Birmingham and Liverpool

Exam tip

When analysing constitutional reforms, make sure you include the reasons for which they were introduced so that you can make a judgement about how successful they have been.

Exam tip

When analysing constitutional reform in general, always have as many examples as possible to illustrate your answers.

Devolution

Before looking at specific details of devolution you should understand what devolution in general means. The following features and principles apply.

- Devolution is a process, not an event. This means that it can continue over a long period of time.
- Devolution refers to the transfer of powers from central government and parliament to regional authorities.
- What is being transferred is power and not sovereignty. The UK Parliament remains sovereign, the ultimate source of all power. Devolved powers can be reclaimed by the UK Parliament and the devolved governments must apply to the UK Parliament for any further transfer of powers.
- Devolution is described as *asymmetric*. This means that the amount of power being transferred to regions can vary from one region to another. Thus Scotland has more autonomous powers than Wales or Northern Ireland. In a true *federal* system, as in the USA, the amount of sovereignty granted to regions is equal.
- Where devolved powers have been approved by a referendum, they are effectively entrenched. This implies that another referendum would be needed to remove them.
- Devolution should not be confused with federalism, as in the USA and Germany, where sovereignty is divided and it requires a constitutional amendment to change the distribution of sovereignty.
- Devolution has three elements: administrative, legislative and financial. These are described in Table 5.

Autonomy/autonomous The term autonomy means that a region or body has a certain degree of its own power but this is short of full **independence**.

Independence In constitutional terms, independence implies that a state or region has its own ultimate powers which cannot be overruled by any other body. In relation to a state it also means full sovereignty.

Table 5 Three types of devolution

Type of devolution	Description	How it applies in the UK
Administrative	The power to determine how services are run and the responsibility to run them within principles set by central government	All three national regions have wide administrative powers and responsibilities over such services as health, education, transport, policing and social services.
Legislative	The power to make primary legislation (fundamental laws)	Scotland and Northern Ireland have this power. Wales did not in 2017 but may apply for such power in the future.
Financial	The power to levy taxes and to spend the proceeds of taxation autonomously	Scotland had very limited financial power after 1998, but has had considerably more financial autonomy since 2016. Wales and Northern Ireland do not have such power.

Devolution and federalism

It is important to distinguish between devolution and federalism. The key issue is where sovereignty lies. In devolution it remains firmly with the UK Parliament, but in a federal system, sovereignty is divided. Table 6 summarises the distinctions.

Federalism A system where regional bodies are granted sovereign powers which cannot be overruled by central government.

Table 6 Distinctions between federalism and devolution

Federalism	Devolution
Legal sovereignty is divided between central government and regional governments. In the USA these are the 50 states.	Power but not sovereignty is delegated from central government to regional governments. Sovereignty remains with a central authority — the Westminster Parliament in the UK.
Federalism is entrenched in a constitution. There has to be a constitutional amendment to change federal arrangements.	Devolution is not entrenched and is therefore flexible.
The powers granted to regional governments are equal and symmetrical. All regional governments have the same powers.	Powers may be delegated in unequal amounts to various regional governments. This is the case in the UK.
Any powers not specified in the constitution are normally granted to regional governments.	Any powers not specified in devolution legislation are reserved to central government.

Devolution in England

This has two elements:

1 **Devolution to English regional authorities (regional devolution).** On the whole, regional devolution has failed but there are now elected mayors in several city regions with some powers over policing, transport, planning and housing.

2 **Autonomous powers for England as opposed to the three national regions (English devolution).** This is limited to English Votes for English Laws (EVEL). When English-only matters are being considered by the Westminster Parliament, MPs representing Welsh, Scottish and Northern Irish constituencies withdraw and take no part.

Scottish devolution

The Scottish Parliament and government have the following powers:

- Power over the health service
- Power over education
- Power over roads and public transport
- Power to make criminal and civil law
- Power over policing
- Power over local authority services
- Regulation of energy industries
- Control over a range of welfare services including housing and disability
- Control of half the receipts from VAT collected in Scotland
- Control over income tax rates and over all receipts from income tax
- Control over air passenger duty and over its revenue
- Control over some business taxes

Exam tip

You do not need to remember all the powers enjoyed by devolved governments. However, you should know three or four examples and certainly know what the devolved financial powers are.

Exam tip

When examining whether the UK is now effectively a federal system, you will find the phrase 'quasi-federal' useful. This means that, although the system is not strictly speaking or legally federal, it is very close to being federal and is effectively federal to all intents and purposes because it will probably never be amended.

Welsh devolution

The Welsh Assembly and government have the following powers:

- Power over the health service
- Power over education
- Power over a variety of local authority services
- Power to regulate public transport
- Power over agricultural regulation and support
- Some control over taxes, including business tax, stamp duty on property sales and landfill tax
- Power to borrow money on open markets to fund infrastructure projects such as roads and hospitals
- Arts subsidies

Exam tip

The powers of the Welsh government are constantly under consideration and may change in the future. You need to keep up to date with any developments.

Northern Ireland devolution

The Northern Ireland Assembly and government have the following powers:

- Power to pass laws not reserved to Westminster
- Power over education administration
- Power over healthcare
- Power to regulate transport
- Power over policing
- Power over the law courts
- Power to regulate and support agriculture
- Sponsorship of the arts

Knowledge check 5

Study the powers granted to the Scottish, Welsh and Northern Ireland governments. Establish which powers are enjoyed by:

- the Scottish government but not the Welsh government
- the Northern Ireland government but not the Welsh government
- all devolved governments

Evaluating devolution

You need to make judgements about how successful devolution has been. Table 7 assesses the different views.

Table 7 An assessment of views on devolution

Positive indications	Negative indications
The United Kingdom has not broken up. A key objective of devolution was to head off nationalist tendencies.	Scottish nationalism is endangering the United Kingdom, especially after the UK voted to leave the EU.
The peace has largely held in Northern Ireland, although the political arrangements remain fragile.	Turnouts in elections to devolved assemblies have been low, suggesting some political apathy.
There remains widespread public support in all three countries for devolution (not reflected in voting turnouts). No serious proposals have been made to reverse it.	The introduction of proportional representation systems has inhibited decisive government in the three countries.
It has made some decisive differences, e.g.: ■ Scotland has no tuition fees. ■ Northern Ireland policing has maintained peace on the whole. ■ Welsh agriculture has been well protected. ■ Social care is free in Scotland. ■ The Welsh health service is improving after several years of decline.	The three countries still have to receive a subsidy from the UK Treasury (the Barnett formula) to maintain their services, in other words they are not yet fully self-supporting.

Debates on further constitutional reform

There have been positive and negative aspects of constitutional reform since 1997. These are as follows:

Positive developments

- The judiciary can now be said to be genuinely independent.
- Through regional and city devolution, power has been decentralised.
- Proportional representation for elections to devolved regional assemblies has improved democracy and representation.
- Elected mayors improve local democracy.
- Citizens' rights are now better protected.
- Freedom of information (FoI) has been established.
- The increased use of referendums has extended popular democracy.
- The House of Lords is a more effective body.

Negative aspects

- The electoral system of first past the post (FPTP) for general elections remains grossly unrepresentative in its outcomes.
- The House of Lords remains an unelected, undemocratic part of the legislature.
- The prerogative powers of the prime minister remain indistinct and largely unconfined.
- The largely unreformed House of Commons remains weak and unrepresentative.
- The UK Constitution remains uncodified, creating uncertainty and lack of public understanding and retaining the danger of excessively powerful government.

Exam tip

When evaluating constitutional reform, remember that it is an ongoing process so include any recent developments and realistic prospects for change.

Prospects for future constitutional reform

Constitutional reform is often described as 'unfinished business'. It is important to understand which future reforms are still being proposed and may move onto the political agenda in the near future. Some of these would complete the task started in 1997. Examples of such unfinished business include:

- The House of Lords may be further reformed to make it either fully elected or partly elected and partly appointed. Either way the remaining hereditary peers are likely to lose their voting rights in the future.
- The electoral system for general elections remains on the agenda. If there is a future hung parliament and more indecisive election results, or excessive unfairness to small parties, the issue may well re-emerge.
- Devolution is a 'process and not an event'. There may well be further transfers of power to Scotland, Wales and Northern Ireland, and possibly even to city regions, in the future.
- The size of the House of Commons is due to be reduced from 650 MPs to 600. This will be accompanied by a redrawing of constituency boundaries to make them equal in population size.
- The Conservatives would like to replace the European Convention on Human Rights with a British **Bill of Rights**. A new set of rights would then be under the control of the UK Parliament instead of the Council of Europe.

Bill of Rights A common name given to any codified set of rights. The USA's first ten amendments to its constitution is known as the US Bill of Rights.

Knowledge check 6

Consider the possible future constitutional reforms listed on page 16. Which of these reforms are most likely to be supported by the following parties?

- The Conservative Party
- The Labour Party
- The Liberal Democrats
- UKIP
- The SNP

The debate over a codified constitution

One of the commonest questions about the future of the UK Constitution concerns whether it should be codified or left in its current form. Table 8 summarises the arguments on both sides of the debate.

Table 8 The pros and cons of codification

For codification	Against codification
It would clarify the nature of the political system to citizens, especially after changes such as devolution and House of Lords reform.	The uncodified constitution is flexible and can easily adapt to changing circumstances such as referendum use and the changing role of the House of Lords. If codified, constitutional changes would be difficult and time-consuming. It can also respond quickly to a changing political climate.
The process of judicial review would be more precise and transparent.	Conservatives argue that it is simply not necessary — the UK has enjoyed a stable political system without a codified constitution.
Liberals argue that it would have the effect of better safeguarding citizens' rights.	As the UK operates under a large number of unwritten conventions, especially in relation to the monarchy and prerogative powers, it would be very difficult to transfer them into written form.
It might prevent the further drift towards excessive executive power (assuming it was also entrenched).	The lack of constitutional constraints allows executive government to be strong and decisive.
It would bring the UK into line with most other modern democracies.	

Exam tip

When evaluating the codification argument, remember that codification also implies entrenchment.

Summary

When you have completed this topic you should have a thorough knowledge of the following information and issues:

- The nature of the UK Constitution
- The sources of the constitution
- The key principles of the constitution
- Constitutional reform, 1997–2010
- Constitutional reform, 2010–2015
- Constitutional reform since 2015
- The nature of devolution
- Distinctions between devolution and federalism
- An evaluation of devolution
- The debate over codification of the constitution
- Possible future constitutional reforms

In addition, you should have gathered appropriate information to help you answer the following wide-ranging questions:

1 To what extent is the UK now a federal system?
2 What does it mean to say the UK Constitution has developed naturally and organically?
3 How successful has devolution been?
4 Why was an extensive programme of constitutional reform launched in 1997?
5 Should the UK Constitution be codified?
6 How successfully was the UK Constitution reformed after 1997?
7 In what sense is constitutional reform 'unfinished business'?

■ Parliament

Defining key terms and principles

Parliamentary government

A key definition is 'parliamentary government'. It is vital to know exactly what this expression means. There are several elements to it, as follows:

- The UK Parliament is the highest source of political authority in the land. Individuals and bodies may only exercise power if it has been sanctioned by Parliament.
- All members of the government must be drawn from Parliament. In practice this means that the prime minister and government ministers must be members of either the House of Commons or the House of Lords.
- Government is permanently accountable to Parliament. Ministers must submit themselves regularly to examination by MPs and/or peers.
- There is no **separation of powers**, as is the case, for example, in the USA. Instead there is a **fusion of powers**. In effect this means that we expect the government to dominate the affairs of Parliament. With a separation of powers, the legislature is separate from government and can exercise control over government.

Parliamentary sovereignty

The word 'sovereignty' means ultimate legal power. When a body is sovereign it cannot be overruled by any other body. In the UK the Westminster Parliament is legally sovereign. This has several elements:

- No individual or body can exercise power unless it has been granted such power by the UK Parliament.

Separation of powers
A constitutional arrangement where there is a separation between the government and the legislature and the two branches have means by which they can control each other's power.

Fusion of powers
In contrast to the separation of powers, this is an arrangement where there is a lack of separation between the government and legislature and where government is expected to exercise control over the legislature.

- Parliament may delegate powers to individuals and other bodies, but it has the legal right to take back those powers.
- The UK Parliament is not bound by any constitutional rules. Indeed Parliament can determine the nature of constitutional rules for itself.
- Each elected parliament cannot bind future parliaments. This means that any laws passed can be undone by a future parliament.
- Each elected parliament is not bound by former parliaments. This effectively means that each parliament can do as it wishes without any restraints.

The erosion of parliamentary sovereignty

Although the UK Parliament remains legally sovereign, in reality a great deal of effective power has moved elsewhere. These are the alternative locations of political sovereignty, or real power.

- Government has political sovereignty. This is for two reasons. First, it has a mandate from the people to govern and to implement its manifesto, as long, that is, that it commands a majority in the House of Commons. Second, we know that the government has various means by which it can control its majority in the UK Parliament. Thus, although the government can be thwarted by Parliament, in reality government has most of the power.
- When a referendum is held, political sovereignty effectively passes to the people. Although the decisions of the people are not legally binding on the UK Parliament (because Parliament is legally sovereign), it is unthinkable that Parliament would not uphold a referendum decision. This was shown in early 2017 when the UK Parliament confirmed the referendum decision to leave the EU even though the majority of MPs were for remaining in the EU.
- Though the European Convention on Human Rights is not technically binding on the UK Parliament, it is understood that the UK Parliament will abide by its terms and will accept the rulings of the Supreme Court on such matters. So this kind of sovereignty lies with the Convention and the Supreme Court.
- Though the devolved governments of Scotland, Wales and Northern Ireland do not enjoy legal sovereignty, it is highly unlikely that the UK Parliament would overrule their decisions or remove their powers, so political sovereignty effectively lies with the devolved governments.

NB Up to the point where the UK leaves the European Union some sovereignty remains in Europe. However, all this legal sovereignty returns to the UK Parliament when the UK leaves the EU.

The structure and role of the House of Commons and House of Lords
The House of Commons and types of MP

The main features are as follows:

- Members of Parliament (MPs) — elected in constituencies (650, soon to be reduced probably to 600)
- Candidates for such elections are selected by committees drawn from local constituency parties.

Exam tip

It is easy to confuse the terms 'parliamentary government' and 'parliamentary sovereignty'. You must, however, be sure to differentiate between the two expressions.

Knowledge check 7

Who *effectively* has sovereignty over these issues?
- Determining UK foreign policy
- Key constitutional changes
- The health service in Scotland
- Determining the true meaning of the 'right to a family life'
- Whether the government can call an early general election

Exam tip

When discussing Parliament, make sure you use the term 'UK Parliament' or 'Westminster Parliament' when you mean Westminster. This differentiates it from the Scottish Parliament.

- Frontbench MPs — government ministers, senior and junior, plus leading spokespersons from opposition parties (about 150)
- Backbench MPs — all those MPs who are not frontbenchers (about 500)
- Select committees — permanent committees of backbench MPs, elected by all the MPs, having various roles including calling government to account (mostly between 11 and 15 members each)
- Legislative committees (also called bill committees) — temporary committees which scrutinise proposed legislation and propose amendments to improve the legislation (mostly 20–40 in size)
- Party whips — senior MPs whose role is to keep party discipline, inform MPs about parliamentary business and occasionally discipline dissident MPs
- The Speaker — elected by MPs, is neutral and keeps order in the house as well as ruling on various disputes that arise over the order and nature of business running through the house

The House of Lords and the selection of peers

The structure is the same as the House of Commons with these exceptions:

- The members are all peers, none is elected.
- There are only a small number of select committees and they have limited importance.
- Bills are not scrutinised by special committees, as in the Commons, but by members of the whole House.

There are different types of peers. These are as follows:

- **Hereditary peers.** They have inherited the title from their father and will pass their peerage on to their sons (a few daughters). There are normally 92 of these peers.
- **Life peers.** Appointed for life by party leaders and an Appointments Commission. They do not pass on their title to their children. In early 2017 there were about 700 life peers. These are a mixture of former politicians and civil servants, other prominent citizens, often retired, political appointees and experts in various fields. Some are there as an honour, others are there in order to take an active part in politics.
- **Archbishops and bishops of the Church of England.** There are 26 of these. No other religions have automatic representation.

While the government normally enjoys the support of a majority of MPs, it rarely has a majority of supporters in the House of Lords. The figures below show the balance of party support in 2016 in the Lords:

Conservative	248	Archbishops and bishops (neutral)	26
Labour	211		
Liberal Democrat	109	Crossbenchers (no party allegiance)	214

Knowledge check 8

Briefly explain the difference between a frontbench and a backbench MP.

Exam tip

Be very careful not to confuse ministers with MPs. Of course most ministers are also MPs, even the prime minister. So ministers have two roles — MP and minister — while backbenchers are only MPs.

Crossbencher A member of the House of Lords who has no party allegiance and is therefore totally independent. There are no crossbenchers in the House of Commons.

The comparative powers of the House of Commons and House of Lords

The functions and powers of the House of Commons

The House of Commons has the following functions and powers:

Legitimation

This is the formal process of making proposed laws legitimate by granting consent. In a sense the Commons is granting consent on behalf of the people. In very extreme circumstances the Commons may reject legislation altogether.

Making government accountable

This key aspect sees the Commons again acting on behalf of the people. Making government accountable means criticising, forcing ministers to explain policy and, in extreme circumstances, it may mean dismissing a government through a vote of no confidence.

Scrutinising legislation

Any proposed legislation is examined by MPs. They may make amendments to improve the legislation and to protect the interests of minorities.

Constituency representation

MPs are expected to ensure that the interests of their constituencies are protected, both the constituency as a whole and individual constituents. This is often done on the floor of the house.

Representation of interests

When the interests of sections of society may be affected by policy, proposed legislation and government decisions, groups of MPs may seek to protect those interests.

National debate

From time to time great issues need to be debated by the representatives of the people. MPs have opportunities to debate such issues.

The functions and powers of the House of Lords

These are more limited than those of the House of Commons:

Revising

This is a shared function with the House of Commons. The Lords scrutinises legislation carefully. The fact that the house contains so many experts makes this process especially meaningful.

Delaying

The Lords cannot veto a piece of legislation but they can force the government to re-present it the following year. This effectively forces government to think again for a year and possibly add amendments to make the legislation acceptable.

Scrutiny The activity of looking at the details of legislation to ensure that it is clear, fair and does not discriminate against minorities.

Secondary legislation

There is a great deal of minor regulation within major laws which has to be approved. The Commons does not have time to review it all so the Lords spends its greater available time checking that it is acceptable.

National debate

This is a function the Lords shares with the House of Commons though its deliberations are less influential.

Limitations on the powers of the House of Lords

The Lords is the junior house (though strangely it is often known as the 'upper house'). This is largely because there are limitations to its powers that the Commons does not have. These limitations are as follows:

- **The Parliament Acts of 1911 and 1949** limited the ability of the House of Lords to delay legislation first to 2 years and then to 1 year. The 1911 Act also prevented the Lords from having any influence over financial matters.
- **The Salisbury Convention**, dating from the 1940s, is a constitutional convention, accepted by members of the Lords. It states that the Lords has no democratic authority to block any proposed legislation for which the government has an electoral mandate (i.e. was contained in its last election manifesto).
- **The amending function is limited.** The Lords can propose amendments to legislation but these will not be enforced unless they are also accepted by the House of Commons.
- **The abolition threat** hangs over the Lords permanently. If, in extreme circumstances, the Lords thwarts the will of the elected government, the government can threaten to bring forward legislation to abolish life peers and replace them with elected representatives or even to abolish the house altogether.
- **Self-restraint is important.** Members of the Lords understand they lack democratic legitimacy and so restrain themselves in some circumstances.

Table 9 summarises the distinctions between the two houses' powers and functions.

> **Knowledge check 9**
>
> What powers does the House of Commons have which the House of Lords does not?

> **Exam tip**
>
> Be careful to establish in your writing whether you are discussing the UK Parliament as a whole or just the House of Commons or even just the House of Lords.

Table 9 The respective functions and powers of the House of Commons and the House of Lords

Powers and functions of the Commons only	Powers and functions of both houses	Functions largely in the House of the Lords only
Examination and approval of the financial affairs of the government	Debating legislation and voting on legislative proposals	Examining secondary legislation and making recommendations for further consideration
Complete veto of legislation in certain circumstances	Proposing amendments to legislation	Delaying primary legislation for up to 1 year
Dismissal of a government by a vote of no confidence	Calling government and individual ministers to account	
Select committee examination of the work of government departments	Debating key issues of the day	
Final approval for amendments to legislation	Private members may introduce legislation of their own	

The legislative process

The passage of a bill from introduction into Parliament to becoming law is a long and complex one. The key stages are shown in Table 10.

Table 10 The passage of a bill through Parliament

First reading	MPs are informed about the bill, or proposed legislation, but it is not debated at this stage. Several weeks normally elapse before further progress.
Second reading	The main debate on the bill. If it is passed it will move to detailed scrutiny.
Committee stage	The bill committee considers the bill line by line and may propose amendments.
Report stage	The bill is debated again with all the passed amendments included.
Third reading	A final debate and a last opportunity to block the legislation.
Passage to other house	Most bills are first presented in the House of Commons so they next pass to the House of Lords. (It can be the other way round.)
Same procedures	Except that the Lords scrutinises with a committee of the whole house.
Royal assent	The formal passage of the bill into law.

The ways in which Parliament interacts with the executive

Backbench members of the Commons

Backbench MPs may be unable to challenge the power of government directly, but they play many other key roles in the political system. These are the main roles played by MPs in the House of Commons:

- Taking part in debates on legislation and voting in divisions
- Speaking in general debates on government business
- Speaking in backbench debates when national or constituency interests can be aired
- Scrutinising proposed legislation at committee stage
- Possibly being a member of a House of Commons select committee
- Active membership of a campaign committee of MPs on a particular issue
- Taking part in fact-finding missions, usually with groups of MPs and often abroad
- Membership of a committee formed by an MP's own party to develop policy on a particular issue
- Campaigning, lobbying and speaking on behalf of an outside interest or cause
- Listening to grievances of constituents against a public body and sometimes acting to try to redress those grievances, including lobbying ministers and government officials
- Attending important events in the constituency, including listening to and perhaps joining local campaign groups

There is a good deal of controversy over how effective MPs actually are. Many of them have poor media and public images. Table 11 summarises an evaluation of the work of MPs.

Exam tip

When considering the effectiveness of Parliament consider both the work of Parliament as a whole and the work of individual MPs.

Table 11 An evaluation of the work of MPs (summary)

Common criticisms of MPs	In defence of MPs
MPs are just 'lobby fodder' or 'party hacks', who simply do as the party whips tell them uncritically and hope their loyalty will one day be rewarded by promotion to ministerial office.	This may be true of many MPs but there are also numerous independent-minded MPs who are willing to put their beliefs and principles above narrow party interest.
Backbench MPs are actually powerless in the face of the domination of the party front benches. They have little or no influence over legislation and fail to bring government effectively to account.	This criticism may have been largely valid in the past, but it is less true today. Especially since 2010, Parliament has been more willing to defy government and the select committees are becoming increasingly effective in calling government to account.
Parliamentary debates are often sparsely attended, suggesting MPs lack interest in public policy.	Much of the work of MPs is carried out behind the scenes, often in committees.
Parliament has very long recesses, giving MPs excessively long, so-called 'holidays'.	MPs often use the long recesses to catch up on constituency work.
MPs are self-seeking and sometimes corrupt, as exemplified by the 'expenses scandal' of 2009–10, when it was revealed that many MPs were claiming excessive, sometimes fraudulent expenses.	MPs have set up systems for controlling such excesses. They are paid a salary which is modest compared to most comparable professions.
MPs are often unknown in their constituencies.	Many, though not all, MPs in fact undertake heavy workloads representing constituency interests, even if they are not well known.

Backbench members of the Lords

There is a wide variety of members of the House of Lords as they come from so many different backgrounds. Many peers also specialise in certain areas of parliamentary activity. Some of the key roles played by backbench peers are as follows:

- Representing sections of society in Parliament, ensuring that their interests are taken into account. Examples of sections of society represented are ethnic minorities, the elderly, hospital patients, the professions.
- Representing important political causes, ensuring they are given as much publicity as possible. These are typically environmental issues, human rights concerns and animal welfare.
- Scrutinising legislation — peers with special expertise play a valuable role in examining proposed legislation.
- Every government department has a frontbench representative in the Lords. This gives peers the opportunity to call government to account, though this receives less publicity than its equivalent activity in the Commons.
- Many peers sit on committees that investigate aspects of government policy and produce reports which may be critical or supportive and may suggest changes to proposals.

Knowledge check 10

Investigate the special field(s) of expertise of the following peers:
- Lord Adonis
- Lord Winston
- Lord Dannatt
- Lord Finkelstein
- Baroness Chakrabarti

The work of select committees

The Public Accounts Committee (House of Commons)

The Public Accounts Committee (PAC) is possibly the most important select committee. Its characteristics are as follows:

- It scrutinises value for money — the economy, efficiency and effectiveness — of public spending and generally holds the government and its civil servants to account for the delivery of public services.

- Its chair is always a member of the main opposition party.
- The chair has great prestige, not to mention an increased salary over other MPs.
- The chair and members are elected by all MPs and so are not controlled by party leaders.
- Its members, despite being party supporters, always tend to act independently, ignoring on the whole their party allegiance. This means the government has no advantage on the committee even though it has a majority on the committee.
- Its reports are often unanimous in their conclusions, so it stands above party politics.
- It has a high profile in the media. Many of its important hearings are broadcast as news items.

Table 12 shows some of its most important reports.

Table 12 Key PAC investigations

Date	Investigation	Conclusion and action
2016	Into the tax affairs of Google	Google's payment of back tax of £130 million for 10 years was considered far too low HMRC should investigate ways of better regulating the tax affairs of multinational companies and making them more transparent
2015	Into the effectiveness of cancer care by the NHS	Highly critical of variations in cancer treatment in different regions and for different age groups Criticised low cure rates and increased waiting times for treatment Publicity caused government to review cancer treatment
2014	Into the financing of fast broadband for poorly served regions	Highly critical of the way in which government financed the programme and for the poor performance of organisations receiving public funds
2010	Into the BBC's use of public funds	Highly critical of poor value for money and lack of accountability by the BBC Recommended government find ways of making the BBC more accountable for how it spends licence payers' money

Departmental select committees (House of Commons only)

Departmental select committees (DSCs) have the following characteristics:

- There are currently 19 such committees, each investigating the work of a government department.
- They scrutinise the work of each department in terms of efficiency, effectiveness, fairness and value for money.
- The members are elected by MPs from the whole house.
- The chair, who receives an increased salary, is elected by the committee.
- Membership varies between 11 and 14.
- The governing party has a majority on each committee.
- The chairs may be from any political party.
- The small parties have a scattering of members.
- Like the PAC, they act largely independently of party allegiance and often produce unanimous reports.
- Also like the PAC, they can call witnesses who may be ministers, civil servants, outside witnesses such as pressure group representatives, or experts.

■ Their reports and recommendations are presented to the whole House of Commons and receive considerable publicity.

Table 13 summarises some important departmental select committee reports.

Table 13 Key departmental select committee reports

Date	Committee	Investigation	Conclusion and action
2016	Work and Pensions	Into the collapse of British Home Stores and the loss of much of the employees' pension fund	The company was reported to the Pensions Regulator.
2016	Business, Innovation and Skills	Into alleged bad working practices at Sports Direct	The company was forced to pay compensation to its workers for paying below the minimum wage.
2015	Treasury	Into proposals for stricter regulation of the banking sector	Insisted that government should implement the recommendations of the Parliamentary Commission on Banking Standards. This pushed policy forward on banking regulation.
2014	Defence	Into the circumstances when the UK should make military interventions in world conflicts	Among many recommendations, urged government to consider legislation about whether Parliament should control major armed interventions.
2012	Home affairs	Into the Independent Police Complaints Commission's (IPCC) role in the investigation into the 1997 Hillsborough disaster	The IPPC is investigating the Hillsborough disaster following the 2016 inquest.

Other select committees in the House of Commons

■ **The Liaison Committee** is made up of all the chairs of the departmental select committees. Twice a year this committee questions the prime minister extensively and sometimes quite aggressively over key aspects of government policy.
■ **The Backbench Business Committee** determines the business of the house for 35 days a year. It decides what will be debated by backbenchers on those days.

Knowledge check 11

Research the Backbench Business Committee. Identify three recent debates established by this committee.

The role and significance of the opposition

While the largest party in the UK Parliament forms the government, the second largest party is the official opposition, also known as **Her Majesty's opposition**, to reflect its official status. The leader of this party is therefore known as leader of the opposition. The other parties form the general opposition. The roles of the opposition are fourfold:

■ To force the government to explain and justify its policies and decisions
■ To highlight the shortcomings of the way the government is running the country
■ To present alternative proposals to those of the government, if appropriate
■ To make itself ready to be an alternative government if the current government is defeated at the next general election

Exam tip

As well as noting the reports in Table 13, you should keep up to date with more recent examples of the work of select committees as they arise. Be as up to date as possible with your examples.

Her Majesty's opposition The official title of the second largest party in the House of Commons. It has a formal role in that it controls a large proportion of the business of the Commons and its leader receives the salary of a government minister.

Calling ministers to account

The UK Parliament calls ministers to account in a number of ways. These include:

- All ministers have to appear before the Commons on a regular basis to answer questions. They may face criticism and will be required to explain and justify policy and decisions.
- Ministers who are peers also have to appear regularly in the Lords.
- Ministers must answer written questions from MPs and peers.
- The prime minister faces prime minister's questions (PMQs) every week. She or he faces questioning by the leader of the opposition and backbench MPs.
- The prime minister is also questioned by the Liaison Committee of the House of Commons twice a year.
- During debates on legislation or general policy, ministers must appear in the UK Parliament to justify the government's position.

Table 14 summarises the positive and negative aspects of the UK Parliament's work and its relationship with the executive.

Table 14 The effectiveness of Parliament assessed

Role	Positive aspects	Negative aspects
Holding government to account	The select committees are increasingly significant. Ministers must still face questioning in both houses.	MPs still lack expertise, knowledge, research back-up and time to investigate government thoroughly. Prime Minister's Question Time (PMQT) remains a media 'event' rather than a serious session.
Providing democratic legitimacy	The UK's system is stable, with widespread consent. Parliament provides strong legitimacy.	The House of Lords cannot provide legitimacy as it is neither elected nor accountable.
Scrutinising legislation	The House of Lords does an increasingly effective job, often improving legislation and blocking unfair or discriminatory aspects of proposals. Experts in various fields in the Lords use their knowledge to good effect.	As legislative committees in the Commons are whipped, this is largely ineffective.
Controlling government power	Increasingly, both houses are checking the power of government especially when the governing party does not have a commanding majority in the Commons.	The power of prime ministerial patronage and control by party whips still means that many MPs are unwilling to challenge the government.
Representing constituents	This is an acknowledged strength of the Westminster system.	It is absent in the House of Lords. MPs' care of their constituencies does vary from MP to MP. There is still no effective mechanism for removing poorly performing MPs.
Representing outside interests	Especially strong in the House of Lords Many MPs, too, support external causes and groups.	When there is a clash between party policy and the interests of groups and causes, party loyalty often wins out.
Representing the national interest	When there is a free vote, both houses are seen at their best. MPs and peers take this very seriously.	When votes are whipped, party loyalty often wins out over national interest.
Acting as a recruiting ground for potential ministers	Parliament is a good training ground for future ministers, demonstrating their abilities well.	Being effective in parliamentary work does not necessarily mean a politician could manage a department of state.

Reform of the House of Lords

There is a great deal of attention paid to the political question of whether and how to reform the House of Lords. Although it is an effective body in many ways, the Lords suffers from a lack of democratic legitimacy. Table 15 summarises the debate on reform. (See also the section on the constitution at the beginning of this guide for more on House of Lords reform.)

Table 15 Arguments for a reformed second chamber

All-appointed	All-elected	Part elected, part appointed
People with special experience and expertise could be recruited into the legislative process.	An elected second chamber would be wholly democratic.	Such a second chamber could enjoy the advantages of both alternatives.
The political make-up of an appointed body could be manipulated to act as a counterbalance to the government's House of Commons majority.	If elected by some kind of proportional representation (PR), it would prevent a government having too much power.	It would increase its legitimacy but retain the services of expert appointed peers.
Without the need to seek re-election, members would be more independent minded.	Under PR, smaller parties and independent members would gain representation they cannot win through FPTP in the House of Commons.	It may be that such a compromise is the only one acceptable to MPs and peers of all parties.
It would avoid the possibility of the same party controlling both houses.	Members of the second chamber would be properly accountable.	

There are few proposals to *change* the powers of the House of Lords, but a reformed chamber might lead to demands for it to have *more* powers. Possible increased powers for a reformed second chamber include:

- the ability to veto legislation, possibly with an enhanced majority
- control over legislation that affects rights and the constitution
- uncontrolled powers of amendment
- the ability to introduce its own legislation

Knowledge check 12

Research the attempt to reform the House of Lords in 2010–11. Establish why the proposals failed.

Reform of the House of Commons

There is little enthusiasm for reform of the House of Commons in the future. However, a number of proposals have been presented or are actually planned. Among them are these:

- The size of the Commons is being reduced, probably to 600 members.
- There have been calls for the departmental select committees to have the power to scrutinise legislation *before* it is debated in the chamber.
- Many MPs would like to see more opportunities to examine secondary (detailed) legislation.
- The key potential reform would be a change to the electoral system to one which is more proportional. This would usually mean that the government would not win an overall majority so MPs would be considerably more independent. In other words, the balance of power between the legislature and the executive would shift towards Parliament. This is an example of an **external** reform.

Exam tip

When considering the reform of the House of Lords, pay attention both to its membership and to its powers.

Summary

When you have completed this topic you should have a thorough knowledge of the following information and issues:

- The nature of parliamentary government
- The nature of parliamentary sovereignty
- The distinction between legal and political sovereignty
- The erosion of parliamentary sovereignty
- The structure of the House of Commons
- The structure of the House of Lords
- The comparative powers of the Houses of Commons and Lords
- The limitations on the powers of the House of Lords
- The nature of the legislative process
- The work and importance of backbench MPs
- The work and importance of select committees
- The role and significance of the opposition

- The debate over House of Lords reform
- Potential House of Commons reform

In addition, you should have gathered appropriate information to help you answer the following wide-ranging questions:

1 To what extent has parliamentary sovereignty been eroded?
2 What are the key distinctions between the House of Commons and the House of Lords?
3 Assess the importance of MPs.
4 Assess the importance of select committees in Parliament.
5 To what extent does the executive control the UK Parliament?
6 Evaluate the arguments for reforming the House of Lords.
7 How effective is the House of Commons?
8 Assess the strength of the opposition in the UK.

Prime minister and executive

The structure, role and powers of the executive

The executive branch of government refers to that part of the political system that directs politics and government. Although the term 'executive' implies the 'carrying out' of policy, in practice the executive also develops policy and legislation. The full role of the executive includes these features:

- The development of government policy
- Conducting foreign policy, including relations with other states and international bodies
- Organising the defence of the country from external and internal threats
- Managing the finances of the state
- Responding to major problems or crises such as armed conflict, security threats, economic difficulties or social disorder
- Controlling and managing the forces of law and order, including the police, courts, armed forces and intelligence services
- Drafting and securing the passage of legislation
- Organising the implementation of legislation
- Organising and managing the services provided by the state

There is no strict definition of what constitutes the executive branch but it certainly includes the following elements:

- The prime minister and her or his close advisers
- The cabinet — 20 to 25 senior ministers appointed by the prime minister
- Various bodies that feed information and advice into the cabinet and to the prime minister
- Government departments — of these the Treasury holds a place of special importance as it controls government finances. Many heads of these departments are members of the cabinet. Others may not be in cabinet but are nonetheless influential.
- The senior civil servants who serve government ministers — of these the cabinet secretary is the most senior. He or she serves both the prime minister personally and the cabinet collectively.
- Various advisers and policy-developing bodies (often called 'think tanks') that serve government departments
- There may also be a few very senior officials of the governing party who hold no official post but who are intimately involved in policy development.

As these elements are the central bodies only, it can also be described as the **core executive**.

The respective roles of the various parts of the core are shown in Table 16.

Core executive The central bodies that together direct the activities of government in the UK.

Table 16 The UK's core executive

Key individual or body	Role(s)	Supporting elements
The prime minister	Chief policy maker and chief executive Head of the governing party	Cabinet Cabinet secretary Chief of staff Private office of civil servants Policy unit
Cabinet	Approving policy and settling disputes within government Determining the government's reaction to crises and emergencies Determining the presentation of government policy	Cabinet committees Cabinet office Cabinet secretary
Treasury	Managing the government's finances Determining the quantity and distribution of taxation in the country	Senior civil servants Special advisers 'Think tanks'
Government departments	Developing and implementing specialised policies for various aspects of the government's responsibilities	Civil servants Special advisers 'Think tanks'

Cabinet committee A small committee of cabinet ministers who formulate proposals for government policy in various areas and present the proposals to the whole cabinet for approval.

Knowledge check 13

Research the current cabinet. Identify three cabinet committees currently operating. Who is the chair of each?

The prime minister and the cabinet

The sources of prime ministerial power

Here we are considering from where the prime minister's power derives. It is not a simple question because the prime minister's is not directly elected (unlike a president, as in the USA). The prime minister power is derived from a number of sources:

- The prime minister is the leader of the governing party and so commands a majority in the House of Commons.
- The prime minister enjoys **prerogative powers**. These are the powers formerly given to the monarch. As the monarch cannot exercise these powers in a modern democracy, they are exercised instead by the prime minister.
- The prime minister is party leader in the House of Commons. This gives him or her a degree of control over parliamentary business.
- The prime minister can claim some authority from the people as he or she has won the previous general election.
- The prime minister is chair of the cabinet and is able to dominate its proceedings.

The powers of the prime minister

These are the main powers of the prime minister:

Prerogative powers

- The prime minister has complete power to appoint or dismiss all government ministers (known as **patronage**), whether in the cabinet or outside the cabinet. The prime minister also has a say in other public appointments, including the most senior civil servants.
- The prime minister has power to negotiate foreign treaties, including trade arrangements with other states or international organisations.
- The prime minister is commander-in-chief of the armed forces and can commit them to action. However, it should be noted that this power has come under challenge in recent times. It is now accepted that the prime minister should only make major military commitments 'on the advice and with the sanction of Parliament'. Nevertheless, once armed forces have been committed to action, the prime minister has general control of their actions.
- The prime minister conducts foreign policy and determines relationships with foreign powers. In this sense the prime minister represents the country internationally.
- The prime minister heads the cabinet system (see below), chooses its members, sets its agenda and determines what cabinet committees should exist and who should sit on them.

Other powers

- The prime minister is chief policy maker. This power derives from the prime minister being the governing party leader.
- It is generally true that the prime minister sets the general tone of economic policy. Usually this is done alongside the chancellor of the exchequer, who is normally a very close colleague.
- The prime minister can speak for the country when abroad or meeting other heads of state.
- The power to call an early general election provided two-thirds of the House of Commons agrees.

Prerogative powers The arbitrary powers of the monarch now exercised on her behalf by the prime minister of the day. The UK Parliament exercises no control over these powers.

Exam tip

The powers of the prime minister are considerable but they must be assessed in relation to the limitations on the powers of the office.

Patronage A key source of power. It means the power to appoint and dismiss ministers, officials and holders of public office. It grants power because those appointed, or hoping to be appointed, owe loyalty to the dispenser of patronage. The UK prime minister has wide patronage power, especially over MPs.

Limitations on the power of the prime minister

Despite the great powers of the prime minister, there are significant limitations to those powers. Some of these limitations vary a great deal according to circumstances. Table 17 summarises these limitations and the circumstances where they are likely to be significant.

Table 17 Summary of limitations on the prime minister's powers

Prime ministerial limitations	Adverse circumstances for a prime minister	Examples
The prime minister may be overruled by the cabinet.	If the cabinet is split or if the prime minister tries to impose a controversial policy	Margaret Thatcher in 1990 when she tried to impose the controversial poll tax
The prime minister may not be able to command Parliament.	The prime minister may have a slim parliamentary majority or lose his or her majority altogether	John Major, 1992–97 David Cameron, 2010–16 Theresa May after 2017
Adverse events may render the prime minister relatively powerless.	Economic crises can cause major problems for a prime minister	Gordon Brown, 2008–10
The prime minister may lose the confidence of his or her own party.	A split in the party can undermine the prime minister	Tony Blair, 2005–2007
Though the prime minister has wide patronage powers, he or she may be forced to appoint to the cabinet adversaries who have a strong following in the party.	If there is a dissident wing in the governing party, which may be held in check if some of its members are promoted to cabinet	John Major, 1990–97 David Cameron, 2010–2015

The concept of ministerial responsibility

Individual ministerial responsibility

Individual ministerial responsibility is a constitutional convention. It has four main elements as follows:

1 Ministers must be prepared to be accountable to Parliament for the policies and decisions made by their department. This means answering questions in the house, facing interrogation by a select committee and justifying their actions in debate.

2 If a minister makes a serious error of judgement, he or she should be required to resign.

3 If a serious error is made by the minister's department, whether or not he or she was involved in the cause of the error, he or she is honour-bound to resign.

4 If the conduct of a minister falls below the standards required of someone in public office, he or she should leave office and may face dismissal by the prime minister.

However, there has been considerable erosion of the principle. In particular, these developments have undermined it:

■ Ministers are no longer prepared to accept responsibility for errors or poor performance by their departments. Unless a major error can be directly attributed to the minister and is very serious, ministers do not normally resign.

Knowledge check 14

Research the poll tax episode in 1988–90. Why was it controversial and how did it lead to Margaret Thatcher's downfall?

Exam tip

When discussing the position of the prime minister, it is important to quote examples of the experience of past UK prime ministers.

- This means that ministers are prepared to lay the blame on lower officials and civil servants. In the past, such unelected officials were protected by the doctrine of ministerial responsibility.
- It is now up to the prime minister to decide whether a minister has to be removed from office under the doctrine.

Table 18 summarises recent examples of ministers losing their posts.

Table 18 Recent ministerial resignations

Date	Minister	Position	Reason
2012	Andrew Mitchell	Chief whip	Allegedly insulting a police officer in Downing Street and using abusive language
2012	Chris Huhne	Energy secretary	Convicted of a serious criminal offence
2011	Liam Fox	Defence secretary	Employing a personal friend as an adviser at the public expense
2010	David Laws	Treasury secretary	Irregularities over his parliamentary expenses claims

It is clear that ministers are far more likely to lose their job over their personal conduct or because they no longer enjoy the confidence of the prime minister than as a result of criticism over their performance as a minister.

Collective ministerial responsibility

The principles of this constitutional convention are as follows:
- Ministers are collectively responsible for all government policies.
- All ministers must publicly support all government policies, even if they disagree privately with them.
- If a minister wishes to dissent publicly from a government policy, he or she is expected to resign first.
- If a minister dissents without resigning, he or she can expect to be dismissed by the prime minister.
- As cabinet meetings are secret, any dissent within government is concealed.

There are a number of reasons why **collective ministerial responsibility** is important:
- It prevents dissident ministers from expressing their views publicly.
- This maintains the image of unity of the government.
- It underpins prime ministerial control over ministers.
- It guarantees a number of votes for the government in any close parliamentary vote. The guaranteed votes of over a hundred ministers is known as the **payroll vote**.

Knowledge check 15

Why was collective ministerial responsibility partially suspended in 2010–15 and during the EU referendum campaign in 2016?

Exam tip

Be very careful not to confuse *individual* ministerial responsibility with *collective* ministerial responsibility. They are very different principles.

Exam tip

Remember that, very often, it is said that ministers have resigned, when in fact they have been sacked. You should try to differentiate between sackings and resignations when using examples.

Collective ministerial responsibility A strong convention that all members of the government, especially cabinet ministers, must defend all government policies in public even if they disagree in private. This maintains cabinet unity and underpins cabinet control by the prime minister.

Payroll vote The guaranteed votes of government ministers in the UK Parliament under the doctrine of collective ministerial responsibility.

Collective ministerial responsibility is a controversial principle. There are both positive and negative aspects to it. Table 19 summarises both sides of the argument.

Table 19 Collective ministerial responsibility evaluated

Positive aspects	Negative aspects
It creates a government which is united, strong and decisive.	Some argue it puts too much power into the hands of the prime minister.
The public, Parliament and the media are presented with a clear, single version of government policy.	It means that ministers cannot be openly honest about their view on policies. This may stifle debate within government.
Though ministers cannot dissent publicly, the confidentiality of the cabinet means that ministers can engage in frank discussions in private.	Resignations under the doctrine are dramatic events which may seriously undermine government.
	It encourages ministers to leak information rather than being open about their opinions.

How prime ministers choose government ministers and the cabinet

Government ministers

The qualities required to be a government minister include these:

■ Loyalty — this is a key quality; prime ministers are reluctant to promote dissidents who challenge the party line
■ Ability to handle difficult situations in Parliament — ministers are constantly being called to account on the floor of the house and in select committees
■ Ability to handle the media
■ Potential ability to manage a large department with many officials and a large budget
■ Popularity within the governing party

Cabinet members

When constructing an effective cabinet, the prime minister may take these considerations into account:

■ Many prime ministers prefer a cabinet which is ideologically unified. This was certainly the case with Tony Blair (1997–2007) and Margaret Thatcher (1979–90).
■ Some prime ministers prefer or are forced into constructing a balanced cabinet with representatives from different parts of the party. This was done by John Major (1990–97) and David Cameron (2010–2016).
■ Increasingly, prime ministers are concerned with the social balance of the cabinet so they promote a good number of women and members of ethnic minorities.
■ One or two ministers should be from the House of Lords so there is senior government representation in that house.

> **Knowledge check 16**
>
> Consider the current cabinet. How many members are women, how many are from ethnic minorities and how many are peers?

The powers of the prime minister and cabinet

We should place the prime minister and cabinet together when discussing power at the centre of government. Between them they control government and direct the political agenda. They have the following powers:

■ They determine the policy of the government.
■ They establish the presentation of that policy.

- They control the agenda of the UK Parliament.
- They determine the priorities of the government, establishing a programme of action.
- Whatever the cabinet declares is policy is binding on the party. This does not guarantee compliance, but it carries a great deal of authority.
- Between them they direct foreign policy.
- Between them they direct economic and financial policy.
- They determine the government's reaction to crises and emergencies.
- They direct any military action taking place abroad.

The relationship between the prime minister and cabinet

The prime minister can control cabinet in a number of ways, including these:

- Patronage is a key element. Because the prime minister solely appoints and dismisses ministers, all members of the cabinet owe him or her their loyalty. The threat of dismissal is a powerful weapon to use against dissident ministers. Prime ministers use patronage to control cabinet and they dismiss and appoint ministers routinely to maintain loyalty. Theresa May cleared out a large minority of David Cameron's former Conservative cabinet in 2016 to ensure cabinet unity.
- Some prime ministers, such as Margaret Thatcher (1979–90) and Tony Blair (1997–2007) used patronage to fill the cabinet with their own close supporters. This means the prime minister can always rely on a majority of support in cabinet.
- Another key element is collective ministerial responsibility. This convention says that all members of the government must defend government policy, even if they disagree privately. If a minister speaks out against government policy, he or she must resign.
- By convention the prime minister controls the cabinet agenda. By determining what cabinet will discuss, the prime minister can avoid opposition and conflict and show preference for his or her own policies.
- The prime minister is closely assisted by the most influential senior civil servant, the cabinet secretary. The cabinet secretary has influence over all government departments and so helps to secure prime ministerial control.
- The prime minister makes appointments to cabinet committees (see above) which discuss and propose policy detail. By manipulating their membership, the prime minister can exert control.
- Most prime ministers maintain an '**inner cabinet**' of close, senior ministerial colleagues who have great influence of their own. The prime minister can control cabinet by reaching separate agreements within the inner cabinet.
- Some prime ministers prefer to reach agreements with colleagues outside cabinet and then present the others with a fait accompli at formal meetings. Under Tony Blair this became known as '**sofa politics**'.

On the other hand, the cabinet can also exercise some control over the prime minister:

- Under unusual circumstances the prime minister can be outvoted in cabinet. Almost certainly, for example, David Cameron was persuaded, against his wishes, to promise a referendum on the UK's membership of the EU after 2015, while Theresa May in 2016 was probably forced by her cabinet to accept that the UK would leave the European single market after exiting the EU.

Exam tip

Remember that relationships in politics are constantly changing according to circumstances. Be as up to date as you can in your knowledge of the position of the respective positions of the prime minister and his or her cabinet.

Knowledge check 17

Research the first days of the premiership of Theresa May in July 2016. How many, and which, cabinet ministers were dismissed in that period?

Inner cabinet A small, permanent group of senior ministers surrounding the prime minister who determine policy outside the main cabinet.

Sofa politics A practice, well known under Tony Blair, whereby the prime minister reaches informal agreements with groups of ministers outside the formal cabinet. David Cameron followed this practice.

- In extreme circumstances the cabinet can remove the prime minister if it loses confidence in him or her. This happened to Margaret Thatcher in 1990.
- Some ministers are virtually 'unsackable' because they would be dangerous if returned to the back benches. This was said of Boris Johnson in 2016–17.
- When the prime minister has no parliamentary majority, he or she must rely more heavily on cabinet support.

Table 20 summarises the relationship between the prime minister and the cabinet, with some examples of how this relationship can play out.

Table 20 Prime minister–cabinet relations

The powers of the prime minister	The powers of the cabinet
The prime minister is perceived by the public to be government leader and representative of the nation. This gives her or him great authority.	If the cabinet is determined, a majority of members can overrule the prime minister.
Prime ministerial patronage means the prime minister has power over ministers and can demand loyalty.	Ultimately the cabinet can effectively remove the prime minister from office, as happened to Margaret Thatcher (1990) and Tony Blair (2007).
The prime minister now has a wide range of individuals or bodies that advise him or her personally.	Cabinet may control powerful ministers with a large following who can thwart the will of the prime minister. Tony Blair was rivalled by Gordon Brown in 2005–07, as was David Cameron by several influential eurosceptics in 2010–15.
The prime minister chairs cabinet and controls its agenda, which means he or she can control the governing process.	If the prime minister leads a divided party it is more difficult to control cabinet. This happened to John Major in 1992–97 and was a constant problem for David Cameron, 2010–16.
The prime minister enjoys prerogative powers and so can bypass cabinet on some issues.	Ministers can 'leak' disagreements to the media and to colleagues and so undermine the prime minister by publicising cabinet splits.
The prime minister can use collective ministerial responsibility to silence critics and hold cabinet together.	

Prime ministerial government versus cabinet government

There are two common descriptions of the nature of government in the UK. One is **cabinet government**, implying that governing is a *collective* exercise. The other is prime ministerial government, implying that the prime minister dominates the core executive. Table 21 summarises the case for each of these descriptions.

Cabinet government A term describing a style of government where there is collective leadership as opposed to the single leadership of the prime minister.

Table 21 Cabinet government or prime ministerial government?

Cabinet government	Prime ministerial government
All domestic government policy has to be legitimised by the cabinet.	The prime minister dominates the political system.
A concerted cabinet can overrule the prime minister.	The prime minister has extensive prerogative powers.
Detailed consideration of government policy takes place in cabinet committees.	The prime minister dominates foreign policy.
The prime minister cannot risk a cabinet revolt and so must consult colleagues regularly.	Collective ministerial responsibility gives the prime minister great authority.
If the prime minister lacks a parliamentary majority.	Prime ministerial patronage commands loyalty.

However, the relationship between the prime minister and the cabinet is not a static one. The relationship will change according to the following circumstances:

- How much authority the prime minister has in terms of his or her parliamentary majority, media image and command over the governing party
- Whether there is ideological unity within the cabinet
- Whether the prime minister has powerful rivals within the cabinet
- How skilfully the prime minister can manipulate cabinet

Exam tip

Keep up to date with developments which illustrate the relationship between the current prime minister and his or her cabinet.

Prime ministerial case studies

Margaret Thatcher

In office: 1979–90

Party: Conservative

Positive aspects
- She won very large parliamentary majorities in 1983 and 1987.
- She enjoyed a mostly positive public and media image after 1982.
- She led a hugely successful military campaign to liberate the Falkland Islands from Argentina in 1982.
- She removed her adversaries from cabinet and led a unified government.
- She developed a strong ideology (neo-liberalism and neo-conservatism) and carried her party with her.
- From 1982 to 1989 the economy improved.
- She won widespread acclaim abroad, especially over her firm stance in the Cold War and her resistance to European integration.
- She faced weak opposition from a divided Labour Party.

Negative aspects
- In her first 3 years she was unpopular and led a divided party.
- A substantial minority of the public actively disliked her.
- She was very stubborn and began to make enemies in her own party.
- The economy began to weaken at the end of the 1980s.
- She made a major error in promoting the very unpopular poll tax, which led to her downfall.

Her fall
In 1989 mounting opposition inside the Conservative Party to her proposals for the unpopular poll tax led to a leadership challenge, won by John Major.

Knowledge check 18

What were the sizes of Thatcher's majorities in 1983 and 1987?

Tony Blair

In office: 1997–2007

Party: Labour

Positive aspects
- He won very large parliamentary majorities in 1997, 2001 and 2005.
- He enjoyed a positive media image until 2003.
- He led two successful military campaigns to liberate Kosovo in 1998–99 and Sierra Leone in 2000.
- He enjoyed a positive image abroad.
- He led a unified cabinet and party.
- He developed a strong ideological position (New Labour and the 'third way') which was supported by most of the party and the whole government.
- The economy improved during his term of office.
- Public services improved under his premiership.
- He faced weak opposition from a divided Conservative Party.

Negative aspects
- The media, especially the conservative tabloids, ran a campaign against him after 2003.
- Members of his own party believed he was accumulating too much personal power.
- His public image was tarnished over Iraq.
- He was challenged by a strong adversary with a large following in the party — Gordon Brown.

His fall
After the failure of the Iraq war to bring peace in the region and amid accusations that Blair had misled Parliament and the public over the causes of the 2003 Iraq war, mounting opposition to his leadership in the Labour Party came to a head and he was forced to resign. Gordon Brown took over.

David Cameron

In office: 2010–16

Party: Conservative

Positive aspects
- He enjoyed a reasonably positive media and public image.
- He was respected abroad on the whole.
- He was able to hold together a coalition government for 5 years, controlling his cabinet successfully.
- Despite having no parliamentary majority, his government lost few parliamentary votes.
- He faced weak opposition from a demoralised Labour Party, which became divided after 2015.

Knowledge check 19

What were the sizes of Tony Blair's majorities in 1997, 2001 and 2005 and what was the role of the 'dodgy dossier' in his ultimate downfall?

Negative aspects

- In 2010 he failed to secure a parliamentary majority and was forced into coalition with the Liberal Democrats.
- In 2015 he only won a parliamentary majority of 12.
- His authority was constantly undermined by the right wing of his own party.
- His party was not ideologically unified. Many did not follow his own progressive, liberal ideas.
- The economy, in the aftermath of the 2008–10 financial crisis, was weak and Cameron was forced to maintain a programme of austerity.

His fall

He had been forced to commit the UK to a referendum on EU membership by the right wing in his own party and the threat of UKIP at the polls. Having fully committed himself to the 'remain' campaign, his position was untenable when he lost the referendum in 2016. Theresa May succeeded him.

Knowledge check 20

Why did Nick Clegg agree to take the Liberal Democrats into coalition with David Cameron's Conservative government in 2010?

What can be learned from the case studies?

There are several common features concerning the position of the prime minister in these cases studies and in the accounts of other premierships.

Positives

- Large or solid parliamentary majorities
- A unified party
- Strong ideological position, well supported
- Weak opposition
- Positive foreign policy events
- Strong economy
- Good public and media image

Negatives

- Lack of a solid parliamentary majority
- A disunited party
- Poor public and media image
- Adverse events
- Weak economy
- Powerful internal party adversaries
- Attempting to dominate excessively, so making enemies

Is the UK prime minister a president?

Finally, you should consider the common question of whether the prime minister is effectively a president. All prime ministers appear to be presidential from time to time, but here you should examine how much substance this has in the long term. The arguments are summarised in Table 22.

Content Guidance

Table 22 Is the prime minister effectively a president?

Yes	No
He or she takes on many of the roles of head of state and speaks for the nation.	He or she is not head of state.
The election of the governing party owes much to the prime minister's leadership.	The prime minister is not directly elected.
Despite parliamentary constraints the prime minister is chief foreign policy maker.	The prime minister's conduct of foreign policy is increasingly subject to parliamentary approval.
Once in action the prime minister makes strategic military decisions.	The prime minister can no longer commit armed forces to action without parliamentary approval.
The prime minister controls the intelligence services at home and abroad.	A prime minister can be removed from office by Parliament or by his or her own party whereas a president cannot.
The prime minister negotiates and agrees foreign treaties.	The powers of the prime minister are not codified in a constitution but are conventional.
Some charismatic prime ministers such as Churchill, Thatcher and Blair have adopted a presidential 'style'.	Prime ministers cannot promote patriotic support for the state to the same extent as presidents often do.

> **Exam tip**
> Remember there is a clear distinction between a head of government (prime minister) and a head of state (president or monarch).

Summary

When you have completed this topic you should have a thorough knowledge of the following information and issues:

- The nature and roles of the core executive
- The nature of government
- The sources of prime ministerial power
- The functions and powers of the prime minister
- The nature and roles of the cabinet
- The nature and importance of individual ministerial responsibility
- The nature and importance of collective ministerial responsibility
- The nature of the relationship between the prime minister and the cabinet
- The extent to which the prime minister controls the cabinet
- The strengths and weaknesses of the office of prime minister
- The nature and importance of the royal prerogative
- Factors in the selection of ministers
- The main features of the performance and experience of three recent prime ministers
- The extent to which the prime minister is effectively a president

In addition, you should have gathered appropriate information to help you answer the following wide-ranging questions:

1. Explain the reasons why the UK prime minister enjoys so much power.
2. To what extent does the UK prime minister control government and Parliament?
3. Assess the importance of collective ministerial responsibility.
4. Explain how, and to what extent, the prime minister controls cabinet.
5. To what extent do the limitations on prime ministerial power now outweigh the strengths of the office?
6. Assess the importance of the cabinet.
7. Explain why some prime ministers seem to be more powerful than others.
8. Is the UK prime minister now effectively a president?

Relationships between the branches

The Supreme Court and judiciary

The top three levels of the UK judiciary are those courts that mostly hear cases of political and constitutional significance as follows:

- **The High Court** hears cases in the first instance.
- **The Appeal Court** hears appeals from cases in lower courts.
- **The Supreme Court** is the highest court of appeal and the final interpreter of law.

The general roles of the judiciary are as follows:

- **Dispensing justice** — hearing criminal cases and civil disputes
- **Making law** — not all law is developed by Parliament, some law is made by judges when they interpret the meaning of law and declare what is 'common law'. This is done through judicial precedent.
- **Interpreting law** — when the meaning and application of law are unclear it is the role of judges to interpret its true meaning.
- **Establishing case law** — judges decide how the law is to be applied in particular kinds of cases. Once established, other courts follow the same case law.
- **Declaring common law** — judges sometimes declare what law should be as we commonly understand it.
- **Judicial review** — courts hear cases brought by citizens, usually against government and the state, when they believe they have been treated unfairly or unequally. Very often these cases apply the terms of the European Convention on Human Rights.
- **Public inquiries** — judges sometimes hold inquiries into matters of major public concern and recommend action to government and the UK Parliament.

Some key public judicial inquiries are shown in Table 23.

Table 23 Recent prominent public inquiries

Year	Name of chair	Subject
2013	Gibson	Into allegations that UK intelligence forces were involved in the torture of terrorist suspects
2012	Leveson	Into the conduct of the press following allegations of widespread 'phone hacking' by journalists in pursuit of stories
2003	Hutton	Into the circumstances surrounding the apparent suicide of civil servant David Kelly, a weapons expert, following questions over his role in the report on Saddam Hussein's so-called weapons of mass destruction
1999	Macpherson	To examine the handling by the police of the case of the murder of black teenager Stephen Lawrence

Judiciary The branch of government that not only enforces the law but also interprets the meaning of law or the meaning of the constitution when they are disputed

Knowledge check 21

Distinguish between the roles of the Lord Chief Justice and the President of the Supreme Court.

Common law Law which is not made by government and Parliament but which exists by tradition, as identified by judges and established by judicial precedent. It often concerns the rights of citizens.

Judicial precedent Judgements by courts which become established in law and must be followed by other courts unless overturned by a senior court.

Judicial review A hearing conducted by a court where a citizen or group of citizens feel they have been treated unfairly, unequally and not according to natural justice by government or any public body. Reviews may reverse decisions and order compensation when they are successful.

The role and composition of the Supreme Court

The Supreme Court was established by the Constitutional Reform Act of 2005. It began to operate in its current form in 2009.

Before the Supreme Court was established, the highest court of appeal was the House of Lords. This operated thus:

- Twelve senior judges sat in the House of Lords as neutral peers.
- When an appeal case was to be heard, five or more of these judges, known as 'Law Lords' would hear the case.
- The head of the Law Lords was the Lord Chancellor, who was a political figure, a member of the cabinet and the head of the whole judiciary.
- Law lords were appointed by the Lord Chancellor in consultation with the government.

The nature and work of the Supreme Court are different. The features of this court are as follows:

- It is still the highest court of appeal in the UK.
- Its members do not sit in the House of Lords.
- Its head is the President of the Supreme Court.
- The Lord Chief Justice heads the judiciary, not the Lord Chancellor.
- The members of the court are appointed by an independent selection commission with no political influence.
- With the UK leaving the European Union, the Supreme Court cannot be overruled by the European Court of Justice.
- However, the court does have a constitutional duty to uphold the European Convention on Human Rights.

Judicial independence and the operation of the Supreme Court

Judicial independence is a key principle of a democracy. It is important for a number of reasons:

- Judges need to be able to enforce the rule of law (equality under the law) without any external pressure.
- Judges hear cases of political importance involving the government itself so they must not be subject to pressure from government if they are to give a neutral judgement.
- Judges must be able to protect the rights of citizens without fear of retribution if they defy government wishes.
- The judiciary is, in some cases, a key check on executive power.

Judicial independence is upheld in a number of ways:

- Judges are appointed for life, so cannot be dismissed if the government disagrees with their judgements.
- Judges cannot have their incomes threatened if they make decisions against government wishes.
- Judges are appointed by a commission which is independent of government.

Knowledge check 22

What was the main recommendation of the Leveson Inquiry?

Exam tip

If you are studying the government and politics of the USA, do not confuse the roles of the UK and the US supreme courts. They have the same name but the US court has enhanced powers because it is backed by the US Constitution whereas the UK court can be overruled by a parliamentary statute.

Judicial independence
A democratic principle that judges should be free from any pressure from government or external forces, that judges should be appointed independently and that they should not fear dismissal as a result of their judgements.

■ It is the duty of government to protect judges from external pressure, for example from the media.

The importance of the Supreme Court can be illustrated by considering cases heard in recent years. These are shown in Table 24.

Table 24 Important cases in the Supreme Court

Case	Year	Legal or constitutional principle	Issue	Outcome
Miller case	2017	On appeal from the High Court. The case concerned the extent of the prerogative powers of government.	Miller, a private citizen, sought a judicial review over the government's refusal to allow the UK Parliament to ratify the decision of the 2016 referendum to leave the European Union.	Miller won the case and the government was forced to allow the UK Parliament to vote on whether the UK should leave the EU.
Schindler v Duchy of Lancaster	2016	The right to vote	Whether UK citizens who had lived abroad for over 15 years should be able to vote in the 2016 EU referendum.	The vote was denied to such citizens as they had forfeited their rights by living abroad for so long.
PJS v News Group Newspapers	2015	Freedom of speech versus the right to privacy	An unnamed celebrity sought to prevent newspapers from printing details of his/her private life.	The court decided that the right to privacy was superior to the freedom of the press without justification for publication.
Trump International Golf Club v Scottish ministers	2015	**Ultra vires** — whether the Scottish government had overstepped its legal powers	Trump argued the government exceeded its powers in allowing a wind farm to be built near his new golf club.	The Scottish government won the case; it had not exceeded its powers.

Knowledge check 23

Research the Miller case in the Supreme Court in January 2017. Why did the Supreme Court rule that there had to be a parliamentary vote on the UK's exit from the EU?

Ultra vires Literally 'beyond power' — a case where it is claimed that a public body has exceeded its legal powers.

The Supreme Court and the executive and Parliament

The Supreme Court and the rest of the judiciary have various ways of controlling the power of both the UK Parliament and the government. In doing so they are preventing abuses of power and asserting the rights of citizens against the state. The methods they use include:

■ The courts enforce the European Convention on Human Rights when interpreting executive actions and in cases of judicial review.

■ The courts cannot set aside a piece of parliamentary legislation, but they can declare that a law is incompatible with the European Convention, which puts pressure on government to amend the law accordingly.

■ Similarly, the courts impose common law, often when asserting the rights of citizens.

- The courts impose the rule of law, ensuring that all citizens are treated equally. This usually occurs as a result of judicial review.
- In cases of ultra vires, the courts decide whether a public body has exceeded its legal powers. This is also the case when judges rule that the government has exceeded its constitutional powers.
- Public inquiries by judges can be very persuasive in forcing government to take certain actions.

Disputes between the senior judiciary and the UK government have become more common. There are a number of reasons why this is occurring. Table 25 shows the root causes and the nature of such disputes.

Table 25 Judiciary–government conflicts

Issue	Detail
Sentencing in criminal cases	The judges wish to have a free hand in determining sentences on a case-by-case basis.
	The government, which is responsible for law and order, insists it needs to impose minimum sentences for some crimes, such as possession of weapons.
Rights	The judges have a duty to preserve human rights, but these may hinder the government's attempts to maintain national security, notably over terrorism.
Freedom of expression	While the government seeks to control the spread of religious extremism, by prosecuting extreme preachers etc., the judges have a duty to preserve freedom of expression.
Freedom of information	The government believes some information should be secret in the national interest, whereas judges view sympathetically appeals under the Freedom of Information Act.
Judicial review	Judges have become more open to hearing appeals by citizens against public bodies which may have acted unlawfully, beyond their powers, have been negligent or have discriminated against certain people.
	Government claims too many judicial reviews inhibit its ability to govern, notably over such issues as the introduction of fracking, airport expansion, new high-speed railways and new road systems.

The Supreme Court (and judiciary) and the protection of rights

How are rights protected?

Courts are crucial protectors of human rights. This occurs in the following ways:

- Enforcing the European Convention on Human Rights
- Enforcing the rule of law
- Asserting common law rights
- Enforcing **freedom of information** cases

Prominent rights cases in recent years are shown in Table 26.

Freedom of information
Enforceable since the Freedom of Information Act 2000, citizens have the right to view information held about them and to view information held by public bodies.

Table 26 Recent rights cases in the Supreme Court

Case	Year	Principle	Issue	Outcome
Brewster case	2017	Whether cohabiting couples have the same joint pensions rights as married couples	Judicial review under the European Convention	Brewster won the case, establishing equal rights for cohabitants.
Evans v *Attorney General*	2015	Freedom of information	Should Prince Charles's letters to the government on various issues be released and published?	It was ruled that the Freedom of Information Act did apply to the royal family's papers.
R v *Metropolitan Commissioner for Police*	2011	Privacy under the European Convention	Whether the police can hold the DNA records of people who have not been convicted of a crime	It was ruled a breach of privacy and thousands of DNA records had to be destroyed.

Who should protect rights and establish justice?

The power of the Supreme Court and the judiciary generally to assert citizens' rights is clear. However, it is a controversial issue whether rights should be controlled by judges or by government and Parliament. Table 27 summarises the rival claims of judges and politicians to protect rights and justice.

Table 27 Judges or politicians: who should protect rights?

Politicians (government)	Judges (the judiciary)
Government is elected and accountable. Judges are neither elected nor accountable.	Judges do not allow political considerations to interfere with their protection of rights.
Government has a clear mandate to govern, and to protect citizens and national security.	As qualified lawyers, judges bring a totally rational approach to questions of law and justice.
Government is able to respond to public opinion.	Because they are not elected, judges can take a long-term view whereas politicians have to consider short-term prospects.

The European Court of Human Rights

UK citizens have the right to appeal to the European Court of Human Rights if they believe their rights have been abused under the European Convention and if they have appealed through the UK courts already but without success. Typical cases involve:

- discrimination on the grounds of gender
- discrimination on the grounds of sexual orientation
- people who have not experienced a fair process of law
- people who have been discriminated against
- UK prisoners claiming their right to vote is denied by UK law

Knowledge check 24

Why was *M* v *Home Office* (1993) such a landmark case?

Exam tip

It is vital to stress, positively and negatively, the significance of the fact that judges are not accountable, while politicians in government and Parliament are accountable.

Knowledge check 25

Look up the case of *McDonnell* v *UK* (2014) in the European Court of Human Rights. What was the issue and what was the outcome?

Table 28 summarises the powers and limitations of the Supreme Court.

Table 28 How much power does the Supreme Court have?

Powers	Weaknesses
The independence of the court is guaranteed in law.	It cannot activate its own cases but must wait for appeals to be lodged.
It can set aside executive actions that contradict the ECHR or the rule of law.	The sovereignty of Parliament means that the court's judgements can be overturned by parliamentary statute.
It can interpret law and so affect the way it is implemented.	The European Court of Human Rights can hear appeals from the court and overturn the decision, but this is not binding.
It cannot overrule the sovereignty of Parliament but it can declare proposed legislation incompatible with the ECHR, which is influential.	
With the UK leaving the EU its judgements cannot be overturned by a higher court.	

Exam tip

Do not confuse the European Court of Human Rights (ECHR) with the European Court of Justice (ECJ). The ECHR still has jurisdiction in the UK whereas the ECJ is part of the European Union and will cease to have any jurisdiction in the UK when the UK leaves the EU.

The relationship between the executive and Parliament

The influence and effectiveness of Parliament

The UK Parliament has the following potential and real powers:

- The UK Parliament is legally sovereign. Its laws and orders have to be obeyed and are enforced by all courts.
- It calls government to account and, if firm enough, can change policy.
- Select committees in the Commons are becoming increasingly influential.
- It can refuse government requests to commit UK armed forces to combat.
- It can, under very unusual circumstances, refuse to agree the government's annual budget.
- It can order emergency debates on key national issues and crises.
- In very extreme circumstances it can veto legislation.
- In some circumstances it can amend legislation against the government's wishes.
- The UK Parliament can, under unusual circumstances, force an early general election by dismissing the government in a **vote of no confidence**.

The power of the executive over the UK Parliament

There are a number of ways in which the executive can control Parliament and a number of structural weaknesses which the UK Parliament has to accept. These are as follows:

- Normally the government enjoys the support of the majority of MPs in the House of Commons. It can expect to win virtually every critical vote. It can usually, though not always, rely on the support of the majority.

Knowledge check 26

When was the last time the UK government lost a vote of no confidence? What were the circumstances?

Vote of no confidence
A vote in the House of Commons which has the effect of dismissing a government and forcing a general election.

- The patronage of the prime minister demands the loyalty of most of his or her party's own MPs.
- The government controls the legislative process and can block most amendments from the floors of the Commons and Lords.
- Collective ministerial responsibility means the government presents a united front to Parliament.
- The House of Lords lacks democratic legitimacy.
- The House of Lords can delay, but cannot veto, legislation.
- The **Salisbury Convention** means that the Lords cannot block legislation for which the government has an electoral mandate.
- Ministers are backed by a huge army of civil servants and advisers, while MPs and peers lack such back-up.

The balance of power between Parliament and the executive

This relationship is constantly changing. Table 29 shows the ways in which the influence of Parliament has been growing in recent years and contrasts them with the ways in which the executive retains its control over the political system.

Table 29 The changing relationship between the UK Parliament and the executive

Factors in the growing influence of Parliament	Factors that retain executive power
Parliament is achieving considerable influence over foreign and military policy. Control over Syria policy is a good example.	Governments still normally enjoy a Commons majority (with the exception of the brief pause in 2010–15).
The select committees are increasingly influential and have come under greater backbench control. They have forced government to reconsider such issues as bank regulation, attacking tax avoidance and evasion, and defence procurement of equipment for the armed forces.	The government still relies on a large 'payroll vote' where all ministers, numbering over a hundred, are bound by collective ministerial responsibility.
The Liaison Committee calls the prime minister increasingly to account. It is a more effective method than prime minister's questions every week.	Government still controls the legislative programme and the Public Bill Committees which propose amendments.
There has not been a decisive government majority in the Commons since 2010.	Prime ministerial patronage still creates loyalty among the government's own MPs.
The House of Lords has become increasingly proactive and obstructive. This is especially true when opposition in the Commons is weak, as has occurred after 2015.	Government still has a huge advantage in resources (advice and research) over Members of Parliament.

It is also true to say that the relationship between the UK Parliament and the executive depends on short-term circumstances. Examples of these circumstances are summarised in Table 30.

Salisbury Convention
A constitutional convention dating from the 1940s. It established that the House of Lords must not block any proposals for which the government has a mandate from the last general election. It is also referred to as the Salisbury Doctrine.

Exam tip

The relationship between government and Parliament is not static. It changes with circumstances. You should keep up to date with changing circumstances.

Table 30 Short-term factors in the UK Parliament–executive relationship

Factors favouring the executive power	Examples	Factors favouring parliamentary power	Examples
A very large parliamentary majority	1983–87 1987–90 1997–2005	A slender government majority or no majority at all	1992–97 2010–15 2015 onwards
Weak and divided opposition	1981–90 1992–2005 2015–	Strong and united opposition	1992–97
A strong economy	1997–2007 1983–88	Economic problems	1990–95 2008–15
A strong, popular prime minister	1982–89 1997–2003 2016–17	A weak, unpopular prime minister	2008–10 2017 onwards
An ineffective House of Lords	1979–99	A strong, active House of Lords	1999–

Exam tip

When using examples to illustrate the changing relationship between the UK Parliament and the executive, try to be as up to date as possible.

The UK and the European Union

The nature of the European Union

The European Union, which dates from the 1950s, was originally an economic union, dedicated to free trade within Europe. However, since its inception it has both grown in size, from six original members to twenty-seven (without the UK), and become a closer political union. It has several aspects:

1 It is a **customs union**. This means that there are no tariffs (import taxes) on any goods and services being traded between member states. It also means that individual member states cannot have separate trade agreements with countries outside the EU. All external trade agreements are common to all members.

2 It is a **free market**. As well as being a customs union, the EU is a free market. This means there can be no barriers to the free movement of goods, services, finance, labour or people between member states. Citizens of a member state are also citizens of the EU and can live wherever they wish within the EU and, broadly speaking, enjoy common citizenship rights.

3 It is a partial political union. There are laws made by the institutions of the EU which apply throughout the union. These mostly relate to trade, consumer protection, development and agricultural subsidies, employment rights and production regulations. These laws ensure that all members compete on a level playing field using the same laws. It also means that the EU collects revenue from members and distributes it in the form of development aid, largely for agricultural and infrastructure development in poorer parts of the EU.

4 Some, but not all, member states are part of a monetary union. This means they use the same currency — the euro.

Customs union An association of states which agree to charge no import taxes (tariffs) on goods and services being traded between them.

European free market Within the European Union, there are no barriers, monetary or otherwise, to the free movement of goods, services, finance, labour and people.

Why UK membership of the European Union was controversial

From the 1990s onwards UK membership of the European Union was a matter of great political conflict within the UK. It split the Conservative Party for decades and created great conflict in other parties, and eventually gave rise to the emergence of UKIP.

The reasons membership of the EU was commonly *opposed* were these:

- The political institutions of the EU were considered undemocratic and especially unaccountable.
- The EU was producing too much 'red tape' and regulation for industry, which was inhibiting progress and imposing excessive costs on business.
- Many felt that the UK was losing sovereignty as the political union of Europe developed.
- It was felt that the UK was forced to contribute more funds to the EU than the value of the benefits it received, i.e. the UK was subsidising less efficient countries.
- The free movement of labour and people was leading to too many migrants entering the UK, putting stress on public services and threatening British 'culture'.
- The excessive subsidising of industry and agriculture was promoting inefficiency.
- It was feared that there was a long-term agenda of creating a 'federal Europe' wherein **national sovereignty** would be lost altogether.

The reasons why UK membership of the EU was widely *supported* were as follows:

- A close union of European states will prevent armed conflict in the future.
- It is widely believed that free trade promotes economic growth and understanding among all the countries involved.
- Europe needs to be a strong power bloc, especially in view of the rise in aggressive Russian nationalism.
- The diversity that comes with free movement of people and labour enriches society.
- The European Union creates a huge market for UK goods and services.
- The European Union will create greater economic equality among all member states.
- The depressed areas of the UK have benefited from EU subsidies.
- UK agriculture has benefited from EU subsidies.
- Workers and consumers are better protected within EU rules.

As we know, the arguments in favour of leaving the EU prevailed in 2016.

National sovereignty
The ability of a country to control its own affairs without external interference.

Knowledge check 29

Research accounts of the 2016 EU referendum campaign. Identify three currently prominent politicians who campaigned to leave and three currently prominent politicians who campaigned to remain in the EU.

Exam tip

The conflict in UK politics over the UK's membership of the European Union was undoubtedly the most important issue in modern history. Be aware that this conflict cut across party lines and so should not be seen in terms of party conflict.

The constitutional and political impact of the UK leaving the EU

Table 31 summarises the constitutional and political impacts of the UK leaving the European Union.

Table 31 The impact of the UK's exit from the EU

Constitutional	Political
The UK will regain full national sovereignty.	There is a new political conflict concerning whether the UK should remain within the European single market.
The European Court of Justice will no longer have any jurisdiction in the UK.	There is continuing political conflict over whether there should be free movement of labour into and out of the UK. This is both within and between parties.
The UK's exit opens up conflict about who should control the UK's future relationship with Europe and the outside world — the government or the UK Parliament.	The political divide between Scotland and the rest of the UK has widened.
There is a continuing conflict over the relationship of Scotland with the EU, given that the Scots overwhelmingly voted to remain in the EU in the 2016 referendum.	It enhanced the authority of prime minister Theresa May, who achieved control over the future trade position of the UK.

The location of sovereignty in the UK

Legal and political sovereignty

In order to understand the location of sovereignty in the UK it is necessary to distinguish between legal and political sovereignty. This is shown below:

- **Legal sovereignty** means ultimate legal power. No other body or institution can overrule Parliament, which has legal sovereignty. The courts will only enforce laws passed by the UK Parliament and will only uphold powers granted by the UK Parliament.
- **Political sovereignty** refers to where power lies *in reality*. Although we know the UK Parliament is legally sovereign, we have to understand that *real* power may lie elsewhere. This is often called political sovereignty.

The changing location of sovereignty

The location of *legal* sovereignty in the UK has changed in one respect — all the sovereignty surrendered to the EU since 1973 when the UK joined is being returned to the UK after 2019.

The location of broader political sovereignty has changed in the following ways:

- Political sovereignty has moved to the devolved administrations.
- Some of the political sovereignty of the executive is shifting towards the UK Parliament. This is particularly true in the areas of foreign interventions and negotiation of foreign treaties.

Legal sovereignty
Ultimate legal power. There is no higher political authority. Legal sovereignty cannot be set aside by any other body or by constitutional rules.

Exam tip

When discussing sovereignty, make sure you state whether you are referring to legal or political sovereignty.

- The increasing use of referendums has transferred political sovereignty to the people.
- The prime minister has lost control over the date of general elections under the Fixed Term Parliaments Act.
- The Human Rights Act shifted control over the enforcement of rights from the UK Parliament to the Supreme Court.

Where sovereignty now lies

It remains true that the UK Parliament is *legally* sovereign. Ultimately, Parliament is **omnicompetent** and can determine how power is distributed in the UK. However, if we look at sovereignty in a broader sense, i.e. political sovereignty, the location of sovereignty depends on the following circumstances:

- In a referendum the people are sovereign even though, technically, the result of a referendum is not binding on Parliament.
- At a general election the people are sovereign because they determine who shall exercise power for the next 5 years.
- For issues which are part of the government's electoral mandate, it can be said that the government is sovereign because it has popular consent for what it is doing.
- With devolved issues, the devolved administrations are effectively sovereign as it is unthinkable that they would be overruled by the UK Parliament.
- When implementing the European Convention on Human Rights, the Supreme Court becomes sovereign.

Omnicompetent A description of the UK Parliament stating that it is able to take any action and pass any law it wishes. There are no constitutional restraints on what the UK Parliament can do.

Summary

When you have completed this topic you should have a thorough knowledge of the following information and issues:
- The nature and role of the senior judiciary
- The importance of the establishment of the Supreme Court in 2005
- The nature and role of the Supreme Court
- The significance of various Supreme Court cases
- An assessment of the power and operation of the Supreme Court
- The ways in which the judiciary can control executive power
- The ways in which the judiciary can protect rights in the UK
- The nature and importance of judicial independence.
- The ways in which judicial independence is established
- The ways in which the government can control the UK Parliament
- The ways in which the UK Parliament can control the power of the government
- The ways in which the balance of power between the executive and the legislature has changed

- The impact of the UK's exit from the EU on the constitution and politics of the UK
- The distinction between legal and political sovereignty
- The changing location of sovereignty in the UK
In addition, you should have gathered appropriate information to help you answer the following wide-ranging questions:
1 How and to what extent can the Supreme Court control executive power?
2 How and to what extent can the Supreme Court protect human rights in the UK?
3 Explain the nature of conflict between the judiciary and executive government in the UK.
4 To what extent can the executive control the UK Parliament?
5 To what extent can Parliament control executive power?
6 Assess the impact of the UK's exit from the European Union.
7 Where does sovereignty now lie in the UK?
8 To what extent has the UK Parliament surrendered its sovereignty?

Questions & Answers

How to use this section

At the beginning of this section is a guide to the structure of the examination for Paper 2, followed by an explanation of the assessment objectives (AOs) and guidance on how to use source material and on timing your answers. It is important that you familiarise yourself with the exam structure, the nature of assessment objectives and how you can score marks for each of those assessment objectives.

There follow some specimen examination questions. These are neither past examination questions, nor future examination questions, but they are very similar to the kind of questions you will face.

The best way to use this section of the guide is to look at each question and make notes on how you would go about answering it, including the key facts and knowledge you would use, the relevant examples, the analysis, arguments and evaluations you would deploy and the conclusions you would reach. You should also make a plan of how you would answer the whole question, taking account of the tips (indicated by the icon ⓔ) immediately below the question.

After each specimen question there are either one or two exemplar answers. There is a strong answer for 10-mark questions and both a strong answer (Student B) and a weaker answer (Student A) for 30-mark A-level answers. The commentary (again indicated by the icon ⓔ that follows it) points out each answer's strengths and weaknesses and gives an indication as to how marks would be awarded for each assessment objective. You should compare these specimen answers with your own notes. Amend your notes to bring them to the standard of the stronger specimen. Having done all this, you can then attempt a full answer to the question, aiming to avoid the weaknesses but including the strengths that have been indicated in the specimen answers and explanation of the marks.

Of course you may use the information in your own way. The above guidance is merely a recommendation. Remember, however, that simply 'learning' the strong specimen answers will not help — these are answers to specimen questions, not the questions you will actually face. It is preferable to learn *how* to answer questions 'actively', that is by writing your own answers, using the questions and answers as a guide. In this way you will be able to tackle effectively any questions that may come your way in the examination.

The structure of the examination

AS Paper 2

Section A: A choice of one from two 10-mark questions.

Section B: Two compulsory 10-mark source-based questions. One question focuses on a single source and the other on two comparative sources. The command word for the first of these questions is 'explain' and for the second 'assess'.

Section C: A choice of one from two 30-mark essay questions. Paper 2 Section C essays have an additional requirement to draw on relevant knowledge and understanding of the study of Component 1: UK Politics.

For examples of 30-mark questions see A-level exemplars. Note, however, that AS and A-level questions have slightly different requirements. AS essay questions always begin with a brief quotation and the words 'How far do you agree…', while A-level questions always begin with the command word 'Evaluate…'. A-level questions also require relevant knowledge and understanding of UK politics and core political ideas.

A-level Paper 2

Section A: One from two source-based 30-mark questions *and* one from two 30-mark essay questions.

Section B is a choice of two essay-style questions about non-core political ideas. **This is not covered in this guide** but is covered in Hodder Education's *Edexcel Politics: Political Ideas Student Guide* (978-1-4718-9313-1).

The nature of assessment objectives

AS and A-level

Assessment objectives refer to the skills and attainment you need to demonstrate to gain marks. They involve knowledge and understanding, analysis, evaluation, constructing a coherent answer, using examples and, where appropriate, using material from different parts of the specification. The latter are known as synoptic skills. A detailed explanation of assessment objectives and synoptic skills can be found in the Edexcel specification.

Using source material

With source questions it is important to make reference to the arguments in each source, to evaluate the different arguments presented in the source and to strike a balance between the different views and arguments in the source. On the occasions when there are two sources for one question, you must make reference to, and analyse, differences between the two sources.

The distribution of assessment objectives

An explanation of how assessment objective marks are attached to each question, plus details of marking levels used by examiners, can be found in the Edexcel specification.

Timing your answers

It is important to allocate an appropriate amount of time to answering each question. How much time you should allocate depends on the proportion of the total marks available for each question. Here we assume 5 minutes' reading time for each of the source questions. On that basis this guide indicates approximately how much time you should spend answering each question, leaving some spare time to look over your answers at the end.

AS

10-mark questions   15 minutes

30-mark question   45 minutes

A-level

30-mark questions   40 minutes

24-mark questions   33 minutes *(not covered in this guide)*

■ AS-style questions

The constitution
Question 1

Describe the nature and importance of constitutional conventions. (10 marks)

ⓔ There should be three parts to this answer. The first part would explain what constitutional conventions actually are. The second would describe some prominent examples. The third, and perhaps most important part, is to explain why they are so important in the operation of the constitution and what is their political significance.

Student answer

It is important in this question to define a constitutional convention. A convention is an unwritten rule or practice that is not actually a law but which is treated as though it is in the political system. There has been much discussion over whether they do have the force of law and it is generally agreed that if a convention is broken it can lead to a constitutional crisis. This is the case with the role of the House of Lords, which is largely conventional. What happens if the Lords decides to defy the will of the House of Commons? The powers of the prime minister are largely conventional because they are really the powers of the monarch exercised by the prime minister. They do not exist in any statutes. **ⓐ**

Some examples can illustrate what they are. There is the Salisbury Convention, which states that the House of Lords must not obstruct any measure for which the government has a mandate, granted to it at the last election, because the measure was in the government's last election manifesto. This is because the Lords is not a democratic body. Another example is the convention that the prime minister is able to appoint and dismiss government ministers. A final example is the convention of collective ministerial responsibility, whereby all members of the government must give public support to government policies. **ⓑ**

The next question is to ask why conventions are so important. The UK Constitution is uncodified, which means that it is inevitable that much of the constitution will be unwritten. They are essential because they make the system work. They are also important because they make the constitution highly flexible. They are also significant in a negative way. **ⓒ** This is that it is difficult to know what the constitution actually is and it leads to disputes about what the constitution says. It is not clear whether they have the force of law, so this causes difficulties. **ⓓ**

So we can see that conventions are important for a number of reasons. One is that they make the system work effectively. Second, they provide a good deal of flexibility in the system and, third, they lead to some disputes about what the constitution actually is.

ⓔ 9/10 marks awarded. This is a strong answer that addresses all three key elements of a good response. **ⓐ** First, it defines constitutional conventions, **ⓑ** then it provides some useful and accurate examples and, finally, **ⓒⓓ** it describes the importance of conventions. This is the answer's only small weakness in that the significance is not fully developed and needs an example to illustrate the issue.

ⓔ All marks are for AO1.

Question 2

Read this original material.

> **The Miller case**
>
> The UK Constitution is neither codified nor entrenched. This means that disputes are bound to arise from time to time about what the constitution means and how it should operate. The Supreme Court is sometimes called up to interpret the meaning of the constitution.
>
> The Miller case, which was heard in 2016–17, was a case in point. The High Court and the Supreme Court both held that the government did not have the power to trigger Article 50 which would start the process of the UK leaving the EU. Instead, the courts ruled, the decision had to be made by Parliament. This ruling firmly established the principle that Parliament is sovereign. It also declared that prerogative powers did not extend to being able to remove the rights of UK citizens. It is important to note that the court was not denying the existence of prerogative powers, but merely asserting that they did not extend to affecting rights. However, there is also a hidden agenda behind the case, which is who should have the final say in any settlement made with the European Union — government or Parliament.
>
> At least the ruling settled the dispute and we now know a little more about the UK Constitution. The government of the day did not agree with the judgement, but had to obey it.

Using the source, explain the significance of the UK Constitution being uncodified. (10 marks)

In your response you must use knowledge and understanding to analyse points that are only in the source. You will not be rewarded for introducing any additional points that are not in the source.

ⓔ You must introduce your answer by explaining what an uncodified constitution actually is and how it works in the UK. Then you should explain its significance. In doing so, you will need to contrast an uncodified constitution with a codified constitution, such as that operating in the USA. It is especially important to explain that the UK Constitution is not only uncodified, but also unentrenched.

Student answer

The source demonstrates that the UK Constitution is above all very flexible. It is uncodified, which means that it has many sources and is not to be found in a single organised document. This also means that it is not entrenched and so it can be changed fairly easily. This is demonstrated by the fact that it needed a judgement by the court to determine what the constitution actually is. In this case it concerns the prerogative powers of the prime minister and the government.

Prerogative powers are the powers which are delegated to the government by the monarchy. These powers are arbitrary and do not need to be approved by Parliament. The prerogative powers include the powers of the prime minister to appoint ministers and grant honours and also to conduct foreign policy. The prime minister is commander-in-chief under these powers. The prime minister can also negotiate and sign foreign treaties. This would include the treaties that keep the UK in the European Union. This means she could also trigger Article 50 that brought the UK out of the EU. It is important to note that Parliament is challenging the prerogative powers to conduct foreign policy and this was illustrated by parliamentary control over action in the Syrian civil war. In this case, though, the case in point was not the power to leave the EU but the fact that leaving would affect the rights of UK citizens and so parliamentary approval was needed. **b** The uncodified nature of the constitution means that disputes like the Miller case and the conflict over Syria will always arise. It also means that the Supreme Court will often be called upon to adjudicate. **c** This makes it doubly important that the Supreme Court is independent of government.

The uncodified nature of the UK Constitution is also significant because it makes it easy to amend. So, if the government wants to clarify or extend its powers it must seek the approval of Parliament, but once it has those powers there is nothing that can be done about it. This is a great advantage because it gives a degree of flexibility but it is also dangerous because it means that government could attach great powers to itself as long as it controls the majority in Parliament. Of course it does not have a majority in the House of Lords so that is an additional safeguard.

In conclusion, we can see that the Miller case illustrates two things about the UK Constitution. The first is that it is not always clear what the powers of the government actually are, in contrast to codified constitutions like that of the USA where such powers are clearly stated. The other illustration is that the Supreme Court can be dragged into what became a very political issue — how the UK would leave the EU after the referendum. **d**

e **10/10 marks awarded.** The great virtue of this answer is that it is aimed at the precise question asked and uses the source to help answer that question. **a** The introductory paragraph demonstrates that the answer is focused on the question. **b** The answer also demonstrates good understanding of the Miller case, the subject of the source. **c** The section also demonstrates excellent understanding of the position of the Supreme Court. **d** Finally, there is a very good conclusion, which summarises the issues well and once again shows understanding of the significance of the constitution being uncodified, the subject of the question.

ⓔ **A01: 5/5 marks, A02: 5/5 marks**

For examples of 30-mark questions see A-level exemplars. Note that 30-mark questions for AS will always begin with a brief quotation and the words: 'How far do you agree…', while A-level 30-mark questions always begin with the command 'Evaluate…'. However, the content of, and approach to, both kinds of question are essentially similar, although the A-level questions also require relevant knowledge and understanding of UK politics and core political ideas.

Parliament
Question 1

Describe the role and importance of departmental select committees. (10 marks)

ⓔ Clearly the answer must explain what the departmental select committees are and what their powers and main features are. Prominent examples of the committees should be described. The main part of the answer should explain their significance. In doing so, some examples of their work should be included. At least two examples would be ideal.

> **Student answer**
>
> The departmental select committees were set up in 1979 to address the problem that Parliament was unable to call government to account effectively enough. Before the committees there was only question time for ministers and this was not working. There are usually 11 members of the committees. In recent years the memberships have been elected by backbench MPs and the chairs are also elected and receive an additional salary. Although the government has a majority on each committee it is expected that the members act in an independent way and often their reports and recommendations will be unanimous. Some of the chairs are also members of the opposition party. **ⓐ**
>
> They have the role of examining the work of a government department. They have the power to call witnesses including ministers, civil servants and advisers and may also examine outside experts and other witnesses. They are concerned about how effectively the department works, they look at how efficient they are and whether their policies are fair and take minorities into account. Sometimes they may be critical because of undue delay. Their style is like that of a court of law and witnesses are often cross-examined quite severely. At the end of an investigation they produce a report to the rest of Parliament. The reports are often highly critical and recommend changes to policy. Ministers and civil servants worry about appearing before them because they may be given a tough time. **ⓑ**
>
> Select committees have produced important reports in the past over the behaviour of the press in the phone hacking scandal which led to the Leveson inquiry, over the supply of equipment to UK troops in Afghanistan and Iraq and over the poor performance of the NHS, especially A & E and over problems in

social care. **c** They can be more effective than the whole of Parliament mainly because they are independent of party whips and because they can focus more clearly and over a long period of time on specific issues.

Their significance is that they do call the government to account more effectively than in the past. **d** There are three main reasons why they are more effective. First, they are very independent and do not behave in a partisan way, second they are taken very seriously by MPs who gain a great deal of personal prestige by sitting on them and third they focus on specific issues and are able to gather a great deal of evidence from witnesses. This means that they are one of the most important aspects of Parliament in the UK today. **e**

e **10/10 marks awarded.** This is a first-class response. **a** It describes select committees extremely well, picking out the most significant elements. **b** Their powers and main procedures are succinctly but well described, followed by **c** a few relevant examples of their work. **e** The answer is effectively rounded off with a summary of their importance and their significance with regard to the work of Parliament in general. **d** A small but significant comment is that they have improved accountability compared to the past, before they existed and before they became more important.

e **All marks are for AO1.**

Question 2 (two-source question)

Read this information.

Source 1

Members of the House of Lords

One of the key features of the mostly appointed House of Lords is the fact that most of its members are experts in a particular field. This is the reason they were originally appointed. Some examples are these:

- Lord Adonis is a Labour peer and former journalist. He has developed special expertise in the fields of transport and education.
- Lord Winston is another Labour-appointed peer. He is an expert in the field of helping childless couples have children through medical intervention. He is also experienced in the area of medical ethics.
- Lord Finkelstein is a Conservative and a working journalist. His field of expertise is politics itself.

- Lord Norton is another Conservative. A professor of politics, he is an expert on constitutional matters.

On the other hand there are many inactive peers and there are still over 90 hereditary peers who owe their position to an accident of birth. There are many peers who are virtually inactive. But the key question is whether such peers are preferable to members who would be elected and therefore accountable. The main problem with such peers is that they lack any form of democratic legitimacy. This means that their position in the legislative process remains ambiguous.

> **Source 2**
>
> ### An elected second chamber
>
> There have been many attempts to introduce an elected second chamber in the UK but all of them have failed. The argument for such a change is compelling. Above all the existing chamber lacks democratic legitimacy and its members are not accountable for their actions. This means it finds it difficult to act as a safeguard against over-mighty government. When a conflict arises between the Commons and the Lords the latter always has to give way. An elected chamber would solve these problems. With greater legitimacy an elected house would feel confident enough to make meaningful amendments to legislation and to hold government to account. On the other hand, it is also suggested that an elected second chamber would have *too* much power and would run the risk of creating deadlock in the legislative process. Such critics prefer the status quo.

Using the sources, assess the arguments in favour of an all-appointed second chamber.

(10 marks)

In your response you must compare both sources by analysing and evaluating them and any knowledge must support this analysis and evaluation in order to gain credit.

ⓔ Some of the answer is given in the sources. The quality of the peers mentioned in Source 1 is a good advertisement for appointed, rather than elected, peers. You must, however, address the question of whether the last hereditary peers should be removed and whether appointed peers are preferable to an elected house. The counter argument — suggesting an elected house — must be examined in order to develop a balanced view of whether an all-appointed house is desirable.

> **Student answer**
>
> Before 1999 most of the House of Lords was occupied by hereditary peers who owed their position to an accident of birth. The minority were life peers appointed by party leaders. This meant that the house was not very professional and that there was an inbuilt Conservative majority. When the house was reformed most of the hereditary peers were removed, all but 92 that is. This means that most of the peers are now appointed and that the government does not have an automatic majority. The house is limited in its powers by the Parliament Acts, which mean it can only delay legislation for a year, and by the Salisbury Convention, which means it cannot block legislation for which the government has an electoral mandate. ⓐ
>
> There have been many calls in recent years for an elected second chamber but these have all failed for a variety of reasons, as Source 2 reveals. The alternative to an elected second chamber is an all-appointed house. This means that all the hereditary peers would be removed and the chamber would be all-appointed. There are a number of arguments in favour of such a house. The main reason is shown in Source 2. Many of the appointed peers are professional people who are experts in a particular field. This means that they can do an excellent job of scrutinising legislation. Because they are experts and representatives of minorities they can improve legislation and make sure that it will work, is clear and protects minority interests. A particularly strong

argument in favour of an appointed house concerns the drawbacks of an elected chamber. Source 2 indicates that there is a danger of legislative gridlock if the second chamber became too powerful. **b**

The issue of accountability is of particular significance. It is perhaps the main reason why an appointed chamber is opposed. Electing members of the second house would solve the problem at a stroke.

As we have said, many say they are not accountable if they are not elected but this matters less than the fact that they can be much more independent than MPs in the House of Commons. The MPs are whipped into line and so become little more than lobby fodder while appointed peers behave independently and can represent minorities which MPs do not. It is also said that they are part of the patronage system of the party leaders, but once they are appointed these leaders have no control over how they behave. It is also true that many of them are crossbenchers, members of no party at all. These are the most independent of all. **c**

Finally, we can also say that an appointed chamber can be a more effective opposition than the opposition in the House of Commons. If they were elected they might simply mirror the situation in the Commons. The sources are correct that they lack democratic legitimacy but they also gain a sort of legitimacy by being independent and by being more able to represent the national interest. It could be said that MPs only really represent the interests of the main parties whom they serve. People like Finkelstein and Norton have much more status and authority than the average backbench MP. Furthermore, such important members would be lost to the legislature in an elected chamber. **c**

e **10/10 marks awarded.** This excellent answer illustrates well how to use the sources and compare them. **a** It begins with a very good setting for the question by looking at the background to House of Lords reform. **b** There follows a thorough exposition of the relevant arguments. This demonstrates a great deal of knowledge which extends from the source without actually straying from it. The unusual strength of this answer is shown by the very good interaction between material from the sources and the student's own understanding. **c** The student clearly understands the points made in the sources but uses them to illustrate a wider analysis. This is analytical ability of the highest quality.

e **AO1: 5/5 marks, AO2: 5/5 marks**

For examples of 30-mark questions see A-level exemplars. Note that 30-mark questions for AS will always begin with a brief quotation and the words 'How far do you agree…', while A-level 30-mark questions always begin with the command 'Evaluate…'. However, the content of, and approach to, both kinds of question are essentially similar, although the A-level questions also require relevant knowledge and understanding of UK politics and core political ideas.

Prime minister and executive
Question 1

Describe the workings and importance of collective ministerial responsibility. (10 marks)

(e) This should be answered in three parts. The first should explain the doctrine. The second should give some examples of when it has operated either negatively or positively, and the third should address the question why it is such an important doctrine, again with illustrations to underpin the arguments.

Student answer

The doctrine of collective ministerial responsibility runs like this: all decisions made by the government are considered to be collective decisions. This means that all members of the government are collectively responsible for them. It also means therefore that all ministers must be prepared to defend and support all decisions made by the government. They may disagree in private, but not in public. If they do disagree they have to resign and go to the back benches or they must face dismissal by the prime minister. (a)

In recent history the most important example of the doctrine at work was when the foreign secretary, Robin Cook, resigned over Tony Blair's decision to join the US invasion of Iraq. Cook accepted that he had to leave the government so he could oppose the policy. He was later joined by the international development secretary, Clare Short, and by some junior ministers. More recently Ian Duncan Smith resigned from the Conservative government in 2016 when he was work and pensions secretary over proposed cuts to disability benefits. (b) It has to be said that there have also been high-profile cases of ministers disagreeing with policy but staying in their job. This has certainly happened with Boris Johnson. (c)

The doctrine is important for a number of reasons. The first is that it underpins prime ministerial control. The prime minister can avoid internal opposition by threatening to sack ministers who disagree. This applies to all ministers not just the cabinet so this means over one hundred people. It also gives the government the appearance of unity even when it might be internally divided. Unity is strength, it is often said, and this certainly gives government great strength. A kind of negative aspect of collective ministerial responsibility is that it prevents proper debate within government although its supporters say there is debate but this takes place in private. Cabinet meetings are secret so we do not know what disagreements there have been.

Collective ministerial responsibility gives rise to the idea of what is called the payroll vote. This means that the government can rely on a hundred ministers all supporting the government in Parliament because their jobs depend on it.

Collective ministerial responsibility was suspended during the referendum campaign over Europe. This was because ministers had to be allowed to campaign openly on either side. This caused a great deal of problems after the vote because some ministers had to support a decision they openly disagreed with. However, it was pointed out that it was the people who made the decision, not the cabinet. (d)

So we can see that collective ministerial responsibility is an important aspect of UK government. It gives the prime minister great power and ensures government unity. The fact that it may be an illusion is not especially important as it is a contribution to stable government. e

e **8/10 marks awarded.** This is a solid answer which covers most of the points. **a** The doctrine is effectively described and **b** two very good examples are used to illustrate its use. The answer does have a weakness, however. This is that it fails to demonstrate the doctrine's importance in relation to ministers who are clearly out of step with the government but remain in the government. **c** The Boris Johnson example is not really substantiated and the point is not developed. There would need to be a brief discussion of how important it is to maintain the stability of government even when there is clear discord within government. The 2 lost marks could be made up by dealing with this issue. **d** Returning to strength, there is a short evaluative section at the end. Evaluation is not rewarded under AO1 but this point does show understanding, which is rewarded here. **e** The final paragraph is a very good summation of the explanation.

e All marks are for AO1.

Question 2

Read this original material.

How prime ministers lose office

It has been said that 'all political careers end in failure'. This was never more true than when applied to UK prime ministers. A look at the demise of several prime ministers can illustrate this point.

Margaret Thatcher, possibly the UK's most dominant prime minister since 1945, was ousted by her own party in 1990. For most of her premiership she enjoyed the backing of a united party and secured large parliamentary majorities. It was perhaps her stubbornness in promoting a highly unpopular reform of local taxation (the introduction of a poll tax) that brought her down. She was defeated in a leadership contest and John Major took over.

Tony Blair, who had come to power on the crest of a wave of hope and popularity in 1997, lost the confidence of the public and his party after the Iraq war of 2003 and its aftermath. Until the Iraq issue brought him down Blair had enjoyed the same advantages as Margaret Thatcher. By 2007 he was forced to retire in favour of Gordon Brown.

David Cameron had to resign in 2016 when he lost the referendum contest over the UK's membership of the EU. Cameron was always beset by difficulties. He had to lead a coalition government in 2010–15 and then only secured a Commons majority of 12 in 2015. The referendum loss was the final straw.

It seems that, however popular a prime minister may be, there comes a point when their power is simply stretched to breaking point. Often, however, this is because they overreach themselves and start making bad decisions. This was certainly true of Margaret Thatcher (poll tax), Tony Blair (Iraq) and David Cameron (EU referendum). After several years in office prime ministers may begin to believe they are infallible.

Using the source, explain the limitations to prime ministerial power.   (10 marks)

In your response you must use knowledge and understanding to analyse points that are only in the source. You will not be rewarded for introducing any additional points that are not in the source.

ⓔ While it seems relatively simple to describe the factors which may limit prime ministerial power, this will not be a complete answer. It is also necessary to explain why these are limitations. Thus, for example, the cabinet can be a limitation, but the real question is how and why the cabinet might remove a prime minister from power.

Student answer

It is usually assumed in Britain that the prime minister is so powerful that he or she is virtually like a US president. Certainly the prime minister's is a powerful office. He or she has wide prerogative powers, enjoys the freedom of the royal prerogative and can usually count on the loyalty of the majority party. The holder of the office is both a party leader and chair of the powerful cabinet. However, we also need to consider the limitations of the office, which may be greater than we think. ⓐ

The source sums up some of the position. Prime ministers with united parties behind them and with large parliamentary majorities tend to hold great power. ⓑ This was illustrated by dominant periods in office enjoyed by Thatcher and Blair. What the source does not tell us is that prime ministers who do not enjoy such a majority and who may lead a divided party are much less powerful. ⓒ It follows that the limitations on the power of prime ministers vary according to circumstances.

The source also refers to what can go wrong for a prime minister. The point of these examples (Thatcher, Blair, Cameron) is to show that the greatest limitations on prime ministerial power concern the cabinet and the party they lead. Thatcher lost the support of the cabinet and was ousted. This shows that the cabinet is a key limit. Blair was brought down by his party, which lost faith in him. Again this illustrates that the party can be a limitation. Events can also turn against a prime minister. This was certainly the case with Cameron, who unexpectedly lost the EU referendum. ⓑ Gordon Brown also lost office partly because of the economic crisis that started in 2008.

A prime minister can only enjoy their considerable powers if the circumstances are in their favour and the source demonstrates this. Adverse events, losing the support of the cabinet, and not being able to carry their party with them, are all key limitations. The source is also implying that the prime minister may prove to be his or her own worst enemy. This is because prime ministers may start to believe that they are completely dominant and this leads them to make serious mistakes. These mistakes may ultimately be their final and fatal limitation. ⓓ

ⓔ **10/10 marks awarded.** This is a very strong answer, which interacts with the source particularly well. ⓐ The context of the question is made clear in the introduction. ⓑ Thereafter the writing makes excellent use of the source, as shown in the two passages marked. ⓒ In particular, the answer demonstrates what is not in the source but might be. **d** The thorough examination of the limitations is well summed up in the final paragraph. This final passage demonstrates the positive use of the source, by telling us not only what it says but also what it implies.

e **A01: 5/5 marks, A02: 5/5 marks**

For examples of 30-mark questions see A-level exemplars. Note that 30-mark questions for AS will always begin with a brief quotation and the words: 'How far do you agree...', while A-level 30-mark questions always begin with the command 'Evaluate...'. However, the content of, and approach to, both kinds of question is essentially similar, although the A-level questions also require relevant knowledge and understanding of UK politics and core political ideas.

Relationships between the branches
Question 1

Describe the work and importance of the Supreme Court. (10 marks)

e It is necessary to explain what the Supreme Court's functions actually are. Having done this, a second aspect to the question needs to be addressed. This is the court's importance. It is essential not just to describe the roles of the court, but also to explain why these roles are important. In order to demonstrate the significance of the court it will be essential to give examples of some of its key judgements.

Student answer

The Supreme Court of the UK was created in 2005 and started its work in 2009. It was an attempt to make sure that the court was even more independent than it had been before. This was because the Law Lords were taken out of Parliament and also because the judges are now appointed independently. We also need to consider what the powers of the Supreme Court actually are. The court can assert our rights by interpreting the European Convention on Human Rights and forcing public bodies to respect its terms. It also considers judicial reviews when there is a suspicion that a body has exceeded its powers or has acted in an unjust way. It is also the case that the Supreme Court can adjudicate disputes about the constitution and the rule of law. It is the country's most senior court and the highest constitutional court in the land. **a**

The Supreme Court has a number of roles and features that make it especially important. The most important role it has is that it hears appeals, which require it to interpret the meaning of law. This happened in the Jogee case **b** when it interpreted the meaning of joint enterprise in homicide cases. In this sense it is important because it is really part of the legislative process declaring what laws mean and how they should be applied (case law). Laws coming from Parliament are not always clear so this is a key function.

Its second key role is that it ensures that the rule of law is maintained. This means that citizens and groups of citizens or organisations can take a case to the court claiming they have been unfairly or unequally treated. As the court is independent it can uphold the rule of law even under pressure from government or from public opinion. Judges are not accountable but they are also independent and it is vital for our human rights that we can rely upon their neutrality. **c**

A third and vital function is to ensure that the government and its ministers do not exceed their legal powers. This is certainly what has happened over attempts by governments to detain terrorist suspects without trial, for which they do not have legal power **d** and over the police's retaining of DNA records of people who had not been convicted of any crime, which is an abuse of the right to privacy. The court ordered these records to be destroyed. **e**

In summary, therefore, we can say that the importance of the Supreme Court lies in three main functions — interpreting laws, protecting rights of citizens and checking the unauthorised power of government. The reason it can do all this is that it has extensive power, being the highest court in the land, that it is neutral and independent. **f**

e **10/10 marks awarded.** This is a strong answer. It has a clear structure — three functions are explained — and makes largely good use of examples. **e** One example is underdeveloped, but **b d** the others are well used. **a** The introduction is very full and sets out the ground well. The answer then follows a logical structure. **c** There is also a good passage on the conceptual position of the court which advances the explanation effectively. **f** Finally, the conclusion summarises the explanation very well, referring to all aspects of the body of the answer.

e **All marks are for AO1.**

Question 2 (two-source question)

Read this original material.

Source 1

Executive dominance

There are a number of ways in which the government can control Parliament. Perhaps the most important is prime ministerial patronage. Rather like medieval kings and queens the prime minister can control the 'court' by promising important positions to anyone who will be loyal. The prime minister is also supported by the party whips.

The party whips have a number of devices to impose discipline on MPs and peers. The main one is an appeal to loyalty. It also has to be said that the government has an electoral mandate to carry out its policies and the whips are quick to remind party members of this democratic reality.

In the most extreme of circumstances a member can be threatened with being suspended from the party or even expelled if they insist on defying the leadership. Most MPs have the ambition of becoming a government minister so the prospect of losing that is a factor in their loyalty.

MPs are more amenable to discipline than peers. Many peers are not professional politicians and are not accountable. This tends to make them more independent than their elected colleagues. Furthermore, while the government normally enjoys the support of a majority in the House of Commons, this is not the case in the House of Lords where no party has an overall majority.

Source 2

Reserve powers

Analyses of the House of Commons often omit one key fact. This is that Parliament enjoys very significant reserve powers. Reserve powers are those which are not used very often, if at all, but which exist in case of unusual and dangerous circumstances. The two main reserve powers are to veto legislation and, in very extreme circumstances, to dismiss a government through a vote of no confidence, something that has not happened since 1979. The fact that these powers are rarely exercised is less important than the fact, of which governments are well aware, that they exist and could be used if necessary. Thus, in a hidden kind of way, they do act as a counterbalance to executive dominance. Governments know that, if they seek to overreach their power beyond their mandate, they are liable to be checked by Parliament.

Using the sources, assess the executive's ability to dominate Parliament in the UK.   (10 marks)

In your response you must compare both sources by analysing and evaluating them and any knowledge must support this analysis and evaluation in order to gain credit.

ⓔ Much of the answer can be found in the sources. However, there needs to be a general analysis of why the executive is dominant. For example, the doctrine of mandate and manifesto should be explained, there should be further explanation of patronage and the inferior status of the House of Lords should be explained. Following that analysis it is necessary to balance the issues raised in the first source against those raised in the second source to give an overall, balanced view.

Student answer

The constitution of the UK has for many years worked in such a way that the executive branch of government is able to dominate the legislature. This is in contrast to systems where there are checks and balances and the legislature can fend for itself and defy the executive. This is very much the case in the USA. It should be no surprise therefore that the government dominates Parliament. ⓐ

Source 1 identifies three ways in which the executive dominates. These are prime ministerial patronage, party loyalty and the activities of the party whips. These are certainly the main reasons for the domination, but there are also other matters to consider. In particular we can say that the elected government has a mandate to carry out its policies so Parliament does not have the legitimacy to defy this mandate. This is especially true of the House of Lords where the Salisbury Doctrine — a constitutional convention — states that the Lords must not obstruct the government's democratic mandate. ⓑ

What is not fully explained is that the domination of Parliament by government depends upon a parliamentary majority. When there is no majority (2010–15) or when there is a very small majority (1992–97 and after 2015) the dominance is much weaker. The principles described in Source 1 are still true but they are less significant. ⓒ When there is a very big majority of the kind enjoyed by Blair and Thatcher we see the complete domination of Parliament.

In addition, too little attention is paid to the latent power of Parliament and to the fact that Parliament remains sovereign, as shown in Source 2. Governments may dominate in the normal course of events, but there may be occasions when Parliament exerts its authority. This occurred in 2016 when Parliament insisted on the repeal of reductions in disability benefits and in 2017 when a budget measure to increase national insurance payments by the self-employed was vetoed by a large minority of MPs. All governments know that, if they cannot carry the parliamentary majority with them, there is a danger that Parliament will withdraw its support and call for a general election. d

The House of Lords is constrained not just by the Salisbury Convention, but also by the Parliament Acts, which means it can only delay legislation and its proposed amendments have to be approved by the Commons, which is, of course, dominated by the executive. This occurred in 2017 when the House of Lords tried to amend the Brexit Bill but had to bow to the authority of the government and the Commons.

So the dominance is not complete, of course, in that Parliament does have the legal power to veto legislation and can ultimately dismiss a government, but these are rare occasions. d In the main we do not expect Parliament to defy government. The government, it could be said, represents the national interest, but Parliament represents mostly local and sectional interests.

In summary, we can say that there are both constitutional and political explanations for the dominance of Parliament by the executive. This may be changing, but the reality is still permanent. e

e **9/10 marks awarded.** This is a strong answer with **a** a good introduction, which adopts a useful conceptual approach (often a good idea in introductions) and **b** **c** good extensions from the source. Good knowledge is shown of such important facts as the Parliament Acts and the Salisbury Convention. Possibly the source material concerning whips needs some more extended discussion but there is generally good interaction with the sources. **d** The student introduces the second source very well and makes comparisons between the two arguments in the sources. **e** The conclusion is a little skimpy. A slightly fuller summary would have been useful. A mark is lost on AO2 for this slightly weak concluding section.

e **AO1: 5/5 marks, AO2: 4/5 marks**

For examples of 30-mark questions see A-level exemplars. Note that 30-mark questions for AS will always begin with a brief quotation and the words: 'How far do you agree…', while A-level 30-mark questions always begin with the command 'Evaluate…'. However, the content of, and approach to, both kinds of question is essentially similar, although the A-level questions also require relevant knowledge and understanding of UK politics and core political ideas.

■ A-level-style questions

The constitution

Question 1

Read this original material.

> **The effectiveness of constitutional reforms since 1997**
>
> Constitutional reform since 1997 has had four major objectives. These have been:
> - to improve democratic legitimacy and accountability
> - to decentralise power away from central government
> - to provide better protection for human rights
> - to bring constitutional arrangements up to date
>
> The record of these reforms has been mixed. In some cases power has been successfully decentralised, with devolution being the key example. Human rights are undoubtedly better protected since the passage of the Human Rights Act and the Freedom of Information Act. The Constitutional Reform Act of 2005 has also guaranteed the independence of the judiciary. The Freedom of Information Act has also increased the rights of citizens to access information from public bodies and has aided both Parliament and the media in their task of calling government to account.
>
> On the other hand, the picture on legitimacy, representation and accountability is less clear. The failure of significant reform of the House of Lords and the electoral system are serious omissions. Furthermore, the nationalists in parts of the UK complain that devolution has not gone far enough. But it is the nature of the electoral system for general elections that is still causing most controversy. The outcomes of the 2010 and 2015 general elections both provided much ammunition for those who campaign for the introduction of proportional representation. On the other hand, the evidence from many European countries suggests that proportional representation carries significant dangers.

Using the source, evaluate the effectiveness of constitutional reform since 1997.   (30 marks)

In your response you must:
- *compare the different opinions in the source*
- *consider this view and the alternative to this view in a balanced way*
- *use knowledge and understanding to help you analyse and evaluate*

ⓔ The answer should begin with a strong introduction which will explain why the programme of constitutional reform was undertaken in 1997. The evaluation should explain which measures have been beneficial in terms of the objectives referred to in the source. It must also look at the weaknesses of the reforms as well as those which are incomplete. The problems with electoral systems would be a key example. The answer should be full of examples of reforms and also evidence as to their successes and their inadequacies. A conclusion should offer an overall assessment of constitutional reform.

Student A

This is an interesting question as it is the most important aspect of British politics since 1997. There were many reforms after 1997 and they have been implemented with varying levels of success and completion. I will be examining four examples of constitutional reform. a

The first is devolution. This was the transfer of large amounts of power to various parts of the United Kingdom, to Wales, Scotland and Northern Ireland. This was not the transfer of sovereignty but merely power. The UK Parliament can reclaim their powers at any time. These countries now have power to control their own transport, healthcare and education plus several other miscellaneous powers. Devolution was popular with the people of these countries, as indicated by the referendums which went before the legislation. b

The second was the Human Rights Act. This brought the European Convention on Human Rights (ECHR) into British law. The importance of this was that it extended human rights in the UK and ensured that government or any other bodies would not be able to abuse people's rights such as the right to life, to free expression, free movement and freedom of religion. The courts will enforce the ECHR. Although it is quite controversial the Human Rights act has proved to be very powerful. b

Third, there was reform of the House of Lords in 1999. This removed all but 92 of the hereditary peers from the House of Lords. It was not as full a reform as people had campaigned for, but it went some way to making the Lords more legitimate. It meant that the Conservatives no longer had a built-in majority and that a whole range of new people with special knowledge and experience could be brought into politics. b

Finally, we have the greater use of referendums. This has extended democracy in the UK because referendums are the purest form of democracy and ensure that the majority has its way. This was shown by the Scottish independence vote in 2014 and the referendum on EU membership in 2016. Referendums bypass the representative system and give a very clear answer to an important issue. b

All these reforms have had a fair amount of success but they have not gone far enough. In particular we have not introduced a codified constitution. A codified constitution would introduce a number of advantages. It would make it very clear what the constitution says and it would help Parliament and the judiciary control the excessive power of government. It would also improve the political engagement of the people. c

As things stand, the constitution is far too vague and flexible. It can easily be changed by any government that commands a majority in the UK Parliament. It therefore follows that constitutional reform cannot be successful until a codified constitution is introduced. d

(e) **13/30 marks awarded.** This is a limited answer in a number of ways. (a) It is clear from the brief introduction that the student is not going to engage properly with the key word in the question, which is 'effectiveness'. Four constitutional reforms are not quite enough. In long, 30-mark answers it is advisable to introduce five or six issues. (b) The descriptions of the four reforms are reasonable, if rather limited. However, the effectiveness of the reforms is assessed only very superficially in each case. (c) The answer then addresses the question of codification, which is of dubious relevance. Above all this answer lacks a thorough evaluation of reforms. (d) The weak conclusion does not really address the question.

(e) **AO1: 5/10 marks, AO2: 4/10 marks, AO3: 4/10 marks**

Student B

As the source indicates, the constitutional reform programme which was instituted in 1997 by the then Labour government had specific objectives. There is no doubt that some of these objectives have been met. Some aspects of reform have been a great success and have been effectively implemented. Critics, however, have argued that the reforms have been less effective than has been claimed and that they are incomplete. This essay will examine both perspectives on constitutional reform. (a)

The jewel in the crown of reform was devolution. At first it seemed to have stemmed the tide of nationalism in Scotland, but a decade later saw the surge in support for the SNP and for greater autonomy. This suggested that perhaps devolution had not gone far enough. As a result of demands for independence Westminster was forced to grant further powers to the Scottish government. Thus the devolution process is ongoing. It has been a success in Scotland, but there are still doubts whether it has gone far enough. In Wales, there were initial doubts about devolution, but in the years since it has become increasingly popular. It seemed that the limited shift in power to Wales was very effective because the Welsh did not want the same degree of devolution as the Scots. Devolution to Northern Ireland was extremely effective as it was adopted to try to cement the peace process. Power sharing has certainly largely brought peace to the province. Democracy has also been well served by devolution because a more democratic electoral system is now used and democratic control and accountability have been brought closer to the people. (b)

The Human Rights Act has certainly furthered the cause of stronger protection for human rights. UK courts now have an effective way of judging whether legislation and acts by public bodies conform to the European Convention and to the rule of law. Critics say it has inhibited the power of the government to protect national security, but this was not one of the objectives of the reform. Hand in hand with it the Constitutional Reform Act of 2005 created the Supreme Court and further guaranteed the independence of the judiciary, a key pillar of democracy. The Freedom of Information Act also extended rights and has made public bodies more accountable. Put together, these reforms have improved the status of rights in the UK, improved democracy, brought democracy closer to the people and modernised the UK political system. (c)

Nevertheless there have been several weaknesses and omissions in these reforms. The failure to reform the House of Lords in a significant way is a serious limitation. It has been effective in improving the quality of membership of the house but has not improved its democratic legitimacy. The UK looks out of step with most other modern democracies.

Turning to the electoral system, the failure to introduce an alternative to first past the post calls into question the UK's claim to be a truly democratic country. The House of Commons remains politically unrepresentative and the government still cannot claim a proper mandate. It is true that PR has been introduced effectively in the devolved systems, but not in the key example of general elections.

Overall, too, there has been no move towards a codified constitution. Such a development would bring Britain into line with virtually every other democratic country. It is also argued that the political system remains too centralised around the executive. A new constitutional settlement could rebalance power in the system towards Parliament. Democracies, some say, need a real separation of powers and a system of checks and balances. This is still absent in Britain. d

Britain is considerably more democratic than it was in 1997; rights are better protected and power has been significantly decentralised towards devolved administrations (a process which is now continuing towards city regions). We can also say that government is more accountable than it used to be and that the UK looks more like most modern democratic states. However, there remain serious problems, notably surrounding the electoral system and the status of the House of Lords. The UK can still not claim to have introduced a fully democratic system. e

e 29/30 marks awarded. This is a strong, thorough answer. a It begins with an excellent introduction, which places the question in context and explains how the student will answer it. There then follows a clear and well-structured analysis with strong evaluation. b Devolution is covered very well and there is plenty of evaluation of this measure. c Similarly, there is a very good review of human rights issues. d The balancing view is also thorough and evaluative. The overall assessment shows good balance between positive and negative aspects of reform. e The conclusion reflects the material in the main body of the answer and gives a good overall assessment with a final firm statement. The only significant omission is no mention of reform of the House of Commons. Although Commons reform is not a central issue, this still loses a mark under AO1 (knowledge and understanding).

e AO1: 9/10 marks, AO2: 10/10 marks, AO3: 10/10 marks

Question 2

Evaluate the view that our human rights are inadequately protected by the UK's constitutional arrangements.

(30 marks)

You must consider this view and the alternative to this view in a balanced way.

ⓔ It is most important in your answer to explain how rights are protected. These will go beyond the European Convention on Human Rights in discussing such issues as the rule of law, an independent judiciary, the importance of common law and the role of the UK Parliament. The more difficult aspect of your answer will be to evaluate rights protection, demonstrating the strengths and weaknesses of v

---

Student A

There are a number of ways in which rights are protected in the UK today. The most important is the fact that the judiciary is independent and has the task of ensuring that the rule of law is preserved. The second way is the imposition of the Human Rights Act after 1998, which means that there is a set of rights that the courts will always enforce. Thirdly we have common law and judicial precedent. These concern rights that have existed for centuries, going back to Magna Carta, and which are confirmed by the courts through judgements that are binding on the courts. At first sight this seems to be a good set of protections, but when we examine the case we can find there are problems with the protection of rights. **ⓐ**

The judiciary in the UK is independent, which means it cannot be pressured into abandoning our rights by government or Parliament. The judges cannot be dismissed by the government and they cannot have pressure placed upon them. There have been many cases when the courts have defied the government and asserted our rights. This has happened more often since the passage of the Human Rights Act. The Human Rights Act is very extensive and covers all the rights that have been established in Europe and in the United Nations. In other words, there are no significant gaps. Any gaps that there might be are also covered by common law and the rule of law and the judges will enforce both if needs be. **ⓑ**

However, the picture is not all optimistic. The most important factor is the sovereignty of Parliament. The UK does not have a codified constitution, which means that Parliament can change it at any time, especially if the government is behind the change. This means that our rights can be taken away at any time and there is nothing the courts can do about it. In countries such as the USA any attempt to tamper with rights may be declared unconstitutional by the Supreme Court. This cannot happen in the UK. In fact there is a strong possibility that a Conservative government in the future will repeal the Human Rights Act and replace it with a British Bill of Rights. This would seem to be satisfactory except that a Bill of Rights may turn out to be weaker than the ECHR. **ⓑ**

If the courts make a judgement that the government does not like or which causes a great storm of public opinion against it, Parliament may respond by simply passing a new law and this will bypass the judgement of the courts. **ⓑ**

We also have to ask whether the courts are truly neutral and independent. Judges are mostly elderly men from a conservative background and so they may well tend to side with the government when there is a conflict about our rights. Judges are supposed to treat all citizens equally and not to discriminate against any groups in society, but in the end they are only human and have the same prejudices as the rest of us. **c**

Turning to common law, this is really too vague to be effective. Parliamentary statutes are clear but common law is certainly not, so citizens are in the hands of judges who are not elected and therefore not accountable to anyone. **d**

How can we evaluate this issue? The answer is really finely balanced. On one side we have an independent judiciary, plenty of legal safeguards such as common law, the rule of law and the HRA, but on the other side we have a powerful executive branch which usually controls Parliament and a Parliament which is sovereign and not limited by a codified constitution. The conclusion, though, has to be that rights are actually well protected as we have had no major issues which have caused widespread dissent. The citizens of the UK are on the whole content with arrangements and have not called for stronger safeguards. **e**

e **18/30 marks awarded.** This answer has a number of virtues. **a** There is a clear and meaningful introduction and **b** there is a good range of arguments on both sides of the evaluation. **e** It also comes to a well-summarised conclusion and is firm in its final judgement. However, it suffers from a major weakness. This is the complete lack of examples. This is demonstrated clearly at **c** and **d** where ideas are introduced but not exemplified. There should be a range of examples of successful rights cases or issues where government has threatened rights. When the USA is correctly introduced we also see no example from that country. A second, less serious weakness is that there are some statements made which cannot be substantiated by evidence. The assertions **c** that judges may not be neutral and **d** that common law is too vague need to be properly examined — they have no evidence to back them up. Answers concerning the role of the judiciary must always contain real examples or the arguments are merely theoretical.

e **AO1: 6/10 marks, AO2: 6/10 marks, AO3: 6/10 marks**

Student B

If we were to look back to before 1998 we might say that it was true that rights were inadequately protected. This was because citizens had to rely on the ECHR, which was nevertheless not binding in the UK, on common law, which can be very unclear, and on parliamentary statutes, which could be amended at any time, especially if the government had a strong parliamentary majority. In addition there were serious questions about whether judges were truly independent of government. Senior judges were appointed by the government and the Lord Chancellor. The Lord Chancellor was, furthermore, a cabinet minister and senior member of the government. There were even questions over whether judges were neutral or whether they favoured some sections of the community. Some argued they were all from wealthy backgrounds, and were white, male and elderly, which was hardly representative of the nation as a whole. Since 1998, however, developments have improved the situation with regard to rights protection. This essay will examine how much rights protection has improved, but also the extent to which rights are still under threat. [a] Since 1998, the position has been transformed. In that year the Human Rights Act was passed. A whole range of human rights were now guaranteed. Every public body had to conform to the European Convention and it was enforceable by the courts. Only Parliament was exempt from this and I will return to this issue later. [b] Whereas before this the ECHR was not binding in the UK, now it was.

The second development was the Constitutional Reform Act of 2005. This set up the Supreme Court and separated the senior judges from the House of Lords. The political figure of the Lord Chancellor was no longer head of the judiciary and the independence of the judiciary was guaranteed by law. This has given the judiciary the opportunity to protect rights in the UK, safe in the knowledge that they would not be under any pressure from the government. Many cases illustrate the power of the judiciary to protect rights. For example, in 2011 the Supreme Court ordered that the police could not hold DNA records of people not convicted of a crime, under the right to privacy. Earlier the senior judges forbade the extradition of radical cleric Abu Qatada on the grounds that the evidence against him was gathered under torture. There have also been many cases of the principle of sex equality being asserted by judges. [c] We can add to this the long-term principle that the judges have always had the task of implementing the rule of law.

It therefore appears that rights are adequately protected in the UK and that the position has been improving. However, there are senses in which the statement that rights are inadequately protected could be justified. [d] The main issue here is the sovereignty of Parliament. Parliament is omnicompetent and so it can remove our rights if it wishes. This is particularly dangerous if the government has a large House of Commons majority. Labour governments under Brown and Blair, for example, with secure majorities were able to threaten rights in the interests of national security. The government can now hold terrorist suspects for 2 weeks without trial, can freeze the assets of suspected terrorists and can view data on mobile phone frequencies. [c] We have also seen vast rises in the use of CCTV, which threatens our privacy. In addition to the sovereignty of Parliament (and therefore government) there is no entrenched constitution, which can force government and Parliament to respect our rights. Virtually all modern democracies have such safeguards, but the UK does not. [d]

The Conservative government is also threatening to repeal the Human Rights Act, which is a huge danger to our rights. It may replace it with a British Bill of Rights, but this would be in the control of the UK Parliament, whereas the ECHR is imposed on the UK externally so we have to respect it.

In summary, therefore, the statement that rights are not adequately protected cannot be sustained. It certainly used to be the case over 20 years ago and it may be in the future, but for now the HRA and the independent judiciary appear to be doing a good job of protecting rights, even though Parliament is sovereign. [e]

e **30/30 marks awarded.** This is an excellent response. **a** It has a very full and very effective introduction, which takes a historical perspective — always a good technique — and sets out the grounds for the answer which follows. **b** There is good organisation, as exemplified at the point marked. **c** The essay makes very good use of examples which act as ideal evidence. **d** The evaluation is clear and strong with a good balance between the statement in the question and the contrary view. **e** The conclusion challenges the statement in the question and this is an acceptable approach provided it can be justified by the evidence presented. This is certainly the case here.

e AO1: 10/10 marks, AO2: 10/10 marks, AO3: 10/10 marks

Parliament

Question 1

Read this original material.

Reform of the House of Lords

After most of the hereditary peers were removed from the House of Lords in 1999 the behaviour and status of the upper house began to change. In that year the House became largely an appointed body. Many of its members are experts in their field and take their role as legislation revisers very seriously. At the committee stage of a bill's passage through the Lords, many peers contribute to improving the legislation. So, although it remains an undemocratic body, the House of Lords could be said to be more effective than ever before.

Nevertheless, calls for its replacement by an elected body remain strong. For democrats it is not acceptable that half the legislature should be unelected and unaccountable. Supporters of this reform ignore the fear that an elected House would fall under the control of party leaderships. As things stand, the Lords is extremely independent of party control and can therefore provide more meaningful opposition and can call government to account more effectively. An elected chamber might also mean that many useful specialists and experts would be lost to politics.

A compromise position is to introduce a part-elected, part-appointed house. Such an option would perhaps provide the best possible solution. This solution seems to be the only one which might command a consensus of support. In the past, even though there has long been widespread agreement that the current composition of the Lords is unsatisfactory, it has proved difficult to establish a solution which can be supported by enough legislators to pass through Parliament successfully.

Using the source, evaluate the arguments in favour of an elected second chamber. (30 marks)

In your response you must:

■ *compare the different opinions in the source*
■ *consider this view and the alternative to this view in a balanced way*
■ *use knowledge and understanding to help you analyse and evaluate*

(e) This is a one-sided question. You are not expected to offer a balanced argument. Rather, you are required to look at the arguments on one side and evaluate them by considering their strengths and weaknesses. In order to do this you need to explain the arguments for an elected chamber. Some arguments are stronger than others and this should be reflected in your answer.

Student A

The issue of House of Lords reform is a very serious one, which has been continuing for many years. This essay will consider the various arguments in favour of and against having an elected second chamber. (a)

There are a number of arguments in favour of an elected chamber. The main one is that it needs to be more democratic and there is no reason why an undemocratic institution should be allowed to make key decisions. Most bicameral systems have some kind of elected second house, so it is important that Britain should conform to the rest of the democratic world. This would also mean that the members of such a house would be accountable to the electorate just as MPs are. (b)

Another reason for an elected chamber is that it would then act as a more effective check on the power of government. At the moment this is not the case. It is a weak house. By having an elected second chamber there would be more opportunities to prevent the government taking extreme measures. Sometimes the opposition in the House of Commons is too weak so it could act as a more effective opposition. (b)

Finally, an elected second house could be elected by proportional representation. This would mean that all parties would have a fair representation in the new chamber. As things stand there is a huge advantage for the big parties, especially the Conservatives, because of first past the post. With a properly representative second chamber all sections of society would be represented. (b)

On the other hand, there are several arguments for retaining an appointed chamber. (c) The main one is that there are many peers who are experts in their field such as Lord Winston (medicine) and Lord Norton (constitutional issues). These people may not stand for election so they would not be in the house at all.

Nevertheless there are drawbacks to an elected chamber. (d) The main one is that the second chamber would become too powerful and if the government did not command a majority there might be deadlock in the system as the Commons would pass legislation which would be obstructed by the Lords. Peers would feel they had a mandate to check the government if they were elected and accountable. Then again, at least many different parties would have a say in legislation, which they do not as things now stand.

If there were too many elections the people may begin to suffer from election fatigue and so turnouts for elections to the second chamber would be low. This would bring into question their legitimacy.

An appointed second chamber would have the advantage that the members would be much more independent minded. If the house was elected, many of the members might be simply 'party hacks'. They would vote the way the whips ordered them. Appointed peers are independent of the whips. [e]

In summary then the arguments for an appointed chamber seem to be stronger than they are for an elected chamber. In particular, such a chamber would be more independent and would carry much more expertise. It would also not be too powerful so there would be less chance of gridlock in the legislative process. [f]

[e] **14/30 marks awarded.** This answer suffers from a major problem. It is really answering a slightly different question. It is comparing an elected chamber with an appointed chamber rather than assessing the various arguments surrounding an elected chamber. [c] Material about the advantages of appointed members can be brought in, but should not have equal status with material about the introduction of an elected chamber. [a] The introduction is very limited and weak and immediately sets off in the wrong direction — a balanced argument instead of an assessment of one side. [b] There are several sound arguments deployed for introducing an elected chamber but none of these is directly assessed. [d] Fortunately, there is a limited overall assessment, but this is not full enough. [e] The interesting comment in the final sentence of the penultimate paragraph should be part of the main assessment, not just an added element. [f] The conclusion is another confirmation that this essay has not addressed the question directly. There are some good marks for AO1, fortunately, because a reasonable range of arguments is demonstrated, but the organisation of the answer is muddled and not focused.

[e] **AO1: 6/10 marks, AO2: 4/10 marks, AO3: 4/10 marks**

Student B

The issue of House of Lords reform is one of the most important constitutional conflicts of modern times. There is general agreement among all the main parties that the Lords needs to be reformed, but there is no consensus agreement on what kind of reform should take place. Several attempts have failed in recent years for this reason. Attention centres on the introduction of an elected second chamber. This is natural as most modern democracies have two elected chambers. The classic model of this is the USA.

This essay will examine the case for an elected second chamber, examining both the strengths and the weaknesses of this argument. In the course of this it will also assess the counter claims of an appointed second house. [a]

The main argument [b] for introducing an elected second house is that it would be democratic. This is obvious. The current arrangement is simply undemocratic. In particular, members of the new house would have to be made accountable if they are allowed to exercise any power at all. This is a very strong argument. However, we must also ask the question of how it would be elected.

If proportional representation were used then it would certainly be a multi-party house, the government would have no guaranteed majority and it might become extremely difficult to pass any legislation at all. This is the experience in the USA and it has a two-party system! Small parties would gain a disproportionate amount of power. It would certainly be a more representative house but how would that help with efficient government? There are also some detailed questions to be asked, such as how long would members serve for? What powers would an elected chamber have? If we give it too much power, this would downgrade the status of the House of Commons and make governing too difficult.

A second, less significant argument c for an elected chamber is that it would give the electorate the opportunity to call the government to account in mid term, always assuming that elections to the second chamber would take place in between general elections. This can be seen in two ways. On the one hand it would enhance accountability, but on the other hand it would give too much power to the electorate. There is a danger that the voters would want to punish a government in mid term so it would become inevitable that opposition parties would dominate the elected chamber. Governments might start to gear their policies towards these mid-term elections. This occurs in the USA where there are mid-term elections.

Finally, c an elected second chamber might have more time to consider legislation thoroughly. The current House of Lords can do this but it has no legitimacy. With real democratic legitimacy an elected chamber might be able to specialise in improving legislation on a democratic basis.

It has to be added that one of the arguments against an elected chamber is that it might be full of lobby fodder, who would simply do as the party whips tell them. The appointed chamber does have independent members who can look at legislation dispassionately. An elected chamber would also lose all the expertise that exists in the current House of Lords. The elected members of a second chamber might have much lower status than the Commons so it would attract representatives of a much inferior calibre.

There is no doubt that an elected second chamber would bring the UK political system into the modern world. It would create a better safeguard against overpowerful government and make the whole political system more representative. These are very strong arguments. However, this must be offset against the problems which might arise, notably the dangers of political deadlock. We would also lose all the advantages of an appointed second house. Prime ministerial patronage, sometimes called 'cronyism', would be reduced but it may simply introduce a fresh army of docile members into the system. In conclusion, therefore, the danger of creating inefficiency and political deadlock is a decisive argument against introducing an elected second chamber. d

ⓔ 26/30 marks awarded. This is a strong and well-focused answer. Above all it does address the question by assessing the virtues of an elected chamber. **ⓐ** The introduction sets the scene for the argument well and then sets out how the answer will follow. There are then three aspects of the question assessed. As is done at **ⓑ** and **ⓒ**, a good technique with assessments is to place the arguments in order of importance. The answer then deals with the alternative of an appointed chamber by linking it closely to the main assessment. Unlike Student A, who compares two alternatives, Student B assesses one of the alternatives. **ⓓ** The summary is especially strong in that it sums up the arguments but also identifies the strongest argument and comes to a firm conclusion. The only weaknesses in this answer are that it pays little direct attention to the source and it fails to discuss the implications of different electoral systems. There should be more material about exactly how an elected system would work and the implications of that.

ⓔ AO1: 8/10 marks, AO2: 9/10 marks, AO3: 9/10 marks

Question 2

Evaluate the effectiveness of backbench MPs. (30 marks)

You must consider this view and the alternative to this view in a balanced way.

ⓔ A good introduction would be to explain that MPs are often criticised for being ineffective and indeed are little more than lobby fodder. The question here is — is this common perception accurate? A balanced answer is required, showing how some aspects of their work are very positive but that they also lack authority and power. In the answer, MPs can be evaluated as individuals and also collectively. The best answer will also explain how the effectiveness of MPs will vary according to circumstances, such as the size of the government's parliamentary majority or whether the government has any majority at all. Some specific examples need to be added.

Student A

A backbench MP is an MP who does not have any ministerial responsibilities. This means on the one hand that they have very little power, but it also means that they have more time to carry out their role as a representative of their constituency. MPs have a number of different roles and they play these roles with varying degrees of effectiveness. It also has to be said that some MPs are harder working than others so we cannot generalise. **ⓐ**

The most important role of a backbencher is to support their party. **ⓑ** They are helped in this role by the party whips. They are elected on the basis of their party's manifesto and they are accountable for that manifesto, so obeying the party whips is part of their democratic duty. Most MPs do this and so could be said to be effective.

The second role is to take part in debates. This is a less effective position. They are not very influential compared with members of the front bench and their opportunities to speak are very limited. Occasionally backbench MPs make great speeches and achieve some status, but this is not normally translated into influence. The party leaders dominate debates and the whips determine the outcome of debates in the form of a division.

Some MPs are lucky to be a member of a select committee and this can be a very important role. They have the chance to question ministers and civil servants and other witnesses and to produce a report that will be considered by Parliament as a whole and which might influence what the government does. **c**

Turning to constituency work, this very much depends on the individual MP. Some spend a great deal of time with constituents, mainly at a weekly surgery. They also answer many letters from constituents and may meet them when they lobby Parliament. They may also speak in parliamentary debates about their constituency and even lobby ministers on behalf of the constituency. In the constituency they may attend important meetings and also major social events.

Finally, we should turn to their most important role which is in the legislative process. **d** MPs sit on bill committees, which consider various amendments that might improve the legislation or might protect the interests of minorities. Here an MP can make a contribution, which may or not be accepted. There is a problem in that the whips will order them how to vote on an amendment but MPs can persuade government that an amendment is advisable.

So we can see that the effectiveness of MPs is extremely variable. It depends on what role they are playing and it depends on the individual concerned. **e**

e **13/30 marks awarded.** **a** The introduction is reasonable but this is a weak response, losing marks on all assessment objectives. In particular, as especially evident at **c**, for example, it does not use any examples. Second, the student is not at all sure of what is the most important role of MPs — at both **b** and **d** the student refers to the most important role. Factors should be placed in order of importance, but this order must be feasible. **e** In common with most of the essay, the conclusion is very limited and poorly developed. The only good feature of this response is that it does raise all the key issues.

e **AO1: 4/10 marks, AO2: 4/10 marks, AO3: 5/10 marks**

Student B

There is a general perception that MPs are little more than party hacks and lobby fodder, that they only do what the party whips tell them to do and play a very limited role in the legislative process. Critics suggest they are almost powerless and that they are not effective in representing local or sectional interests. However, it could be argued that this is an unfair picture. Especially in recent years, backbenchers have played an increasingly important role in the political process. This essay will examine these rival perspectives on MPs. **a**

It is certainly true that for most of the time and in most circumstances MPs are required to follow the party line. This is natural as the governing party has a mandate to carry out its manifesto commitments. Opposition MPs can be more independent as their party is not in government, but they still tend to vote the way the party whips tell them. But the role of MPs is much wider than this and this essay will examine how well MPs carry out these other roles. I will also examine how effective MPs are as a whole, i.e. the whole House of Commons, and how effective they are as individuals. b

Collectively the House of Commons spends much of its time in a ritual process of passing laws proposed by government. Opposition is largely token, and scrutinising legislation is a weak function as the government has a majority on bill committees and the whips ensure that the government will always get its way. The opportunities for MPs to raise constituency matters or to defend sectional interests in the House are very limited. Question times, too, are largely ineffective as ministers and the prime minister find it relatively easy to avoid answering questions fully. However, when we turn to committee work we see a different picture. Having said that, there have been examples of backbench action, for example over cuts to disability benefits in 2016 and rises in national insurance payments by the self-employed in 2017. In these cases the government was forced to do a U-turn. Determined groups of MPs can be effective, especially now when the government has a small majority. c

The MPs who sit on select committees do sterling work in calling government to account. They behave in an independent way and are able to obtain key information from ministers, advisers, civil servants and other witnesses. The Public Accounts Committee has forced government action in recent years on such issues as tax avoidance and evasion, the accounts of the BBC and the financial performance of the NHS. The departmental select committees are especially effective. The Work and Pensions Committee forced Sir Philip Green to pay money into the BHS pension fund and the Business Committee also highlighted bad working practices at Sports Direct. The Health Committee calls the government to account effectively on social care and the health service. d

There have also been examples of MPs defending constituency interests by directly lobbying ministers. This occurred over changes to education spending in 2017 when schools in some areas were losing some of their funding. There has also been lobbying over the introduction of grammar schools.

Collectively, we have to remember that the effectiveness of MPs will very much depend on how secure the government is. Under the Conservative government elected in 2015 with a slender majority, small groups of MPs were able to exercise a good deal of influence as the government could not tolerate even small party rebellions. Naturally, when the government has a big majority, as it did under Blair and Thatcher, MPs become considerably less effective. e

Turning to their role as representatives of their constituency, it has to be remembered that MPs do a great deal of local work. They take up the grievances of constituents and help individuals and families who are having difficulties with such issues as welfare benefits, healthcare issues, asylum and so on. MPs can lobby officials and ministers and are able to use their influence to help. Of course it is inevitable that some MPs are more effective than others in this role. All MPs also defend constituency interests generally when it comes to policy, examples being airport expansion, fracking and hospital closures. One of the factors involved in this is whether the MP has a large majority or sits for a marginal seat. MPs in the latter are bound to work harder for the constituents as they know they will need their votes at the next election. f

In summary, we can say this is a mixed picture. MPs are less effective when the government has a large majority in the Commons. They are also relatively weak in the legislative process in general because of party control. However, when the government lacks a large majority, the picture changes. At constituency level many MPs work extremely hard in dealing with grievances and defending local interests. There are also many MPs sitting on select committees and it is perhaps in these committees that we see the most effective work of MPs. The question is not as simple as it first seems. g

e 30/30 marks awarded. This is a strong answer full of evaluation, knowledge and examples. It is also very good in describing the effects of different contexts (for example, how large is the government's majority). a b The introduction is very strong, setting the scene and laying out how the answer will follow. c d There is very good use of examples, as shown in the third and fourth paragraphs. e f Context, as well as evaluation, appears in paragraphs 6 and 7. g The summary is both thorough and informative. It demonstrates the changing position of MPs and comes to a firm conclusion that select committee work is of most importance. This response has all the elements needed for full marks.

e AO1: 10/10 marks, AO2: 10/10 marks, AO3: 10/10 marks

Prime minister and executive
Question 1

Read this original material.

The core executive

Although it cannot be precisely defined, the core executive contains the following elements:

- The prime minister and her or his close advisers.
- The cabinet. 20–25 senior ministers appointed by the prime minister.
- Various bodies that feed information and advice into the cabinet and to the prime minister.
- Government departments. Of these the Treasury holds a place of special importance as it controls government finances. Many heads of these departments are members of the cabinet. Others may not be in cabinet but are nonetheless influential.
- The senior civil servants who serve government ministers. Of these the cabinet secretary is the most senior. He or she serves both the prime minister personally and the cabinet collectively.
- Various advisers and policy-developing bodies (often called 'think tanks') that serve government departments.
- There may also be a few very senior officials of the governing party who hold no official post but who are intimately involved in policy development.

We can see that a minority of the membership of the core executive is elected. It is also true that, although the cabinet is said to stand in the centre of the executive, it has many rivals in terms of policy formulation. It certainly should be remembered, however, that the cabinet is a clearing house for all important decisions even if they have been made in a different part of the core executive. It has a veto over all such decisions and can overrule the prime minister her- or himself. It is also where internal government conflicts are resolved.

A further perception of the core executive rests with the belief that the prime minister stands at the centre, rather than the cabinet. This is a theory known as prime ministerial government. It is based on the considerable devices the prime minister has at her or his disposal to control members of cabinet, individually and collectively.

Evaluate the importance of the cabinet in policy making. (30 marks)

In your response you must:
- *compare the different opinions in the source*
- *consider this view and the alternative to this view in a balanced way*
- *use knowledge and understanding to help you analyse and evaluate*

ⓔ It is important at the outset to explain what the conventional roles of the cabinet actually are. The strengths and weaknesses of the cabinet should be considered, especially in relation to the power of the prime minister. The answer should also look at the cabinet in relation to the other parts of the core executive. The relationship between the cabinet and the prime minister varies through time and in different circumstances. This should be reflected in your answer, along with appropriate examples.

Student A

The cabinet stands at the centre of the core executive so much so that British government is sometimes described as cabinet government. This is because the key decisions are made at cabinet even though the prime minister has considerable power. This essay will start by describing the role of the cabinet, followed by an assessment of how important it is, followed by the limitations on its powers. **a**

The cabinet has a number of roles. First, it sometimes makes important decisions when there is a crisis or an emergency. Sometimes too it meets as COBRA when an inner group of ministers makes an emergency decision. It is not strictly true that the cabinet makes policies but it certainly makes key decisions. For example, if the UK were thinking about committing troops to combat it would be cabinet that made the final decision. **b**

Second, the cabinet settles disputes within government. These can often be about spending decisions. When two ministers have a dispute the prime minister will attempt to solve it. If he fails then the matter must be brought before the whole cabinet. **c**

Third, the cabinet decides on the government's priorities and controls parliamentary business. It meets regularly every week and at that meeting the future business of the government will be decided. In addition they will discuss current policy and decide how the policies should be presented in Parliament and in the media. The cabinet operates a system of collective ministerial responsibility, which means that all its members must defend the same policies and are not permitted to make any statements which might be seen to contradict that policy. **c**

Fourth and finally, the cabinet is a kind of rubber stamp for decisions which are made elsewhere. Detailed decisions are made by small cabinet committees and by individual ministers. Some decisions are also, of course, made by the prime minister. However, these decisions are not official government policy until they have been approved by the cabinet.

So we can see that the cabinet is an extremely important part of the core executive and stands at the centre of government. It is the collective decision-making organ of the government and draws strength from the fact that it has collective ministerial responsibility. The members are the senior members of the government and the close colleagues of the prime minister. **d**

There are some limits to the decision-making powers of the cabinet. The main one is the control exercised by the prime minister. The prime minister has a variety of ways of controlling the cabinet and the government in general. The prime minister is helped by his own department known as the cabinet office and he has a large number of advisers and think tanks. The prime minister also controls the agenda of the cabinet. This means he can decide what is discussed and what is not discussed. Tony Blair used a system known as sofa politics to keep control. He made agreements with powerful ministers outside the cabinet so when the meeting happened some decisions had already been made.

We must also remember that the prime minister can use patronage to control cabinet. He has full power to appoint and dismiss ministers so in that way he can ensure their loyalty when there is a policy dispute inside government.

Finally we should say that the prime minister has prerogative powers. These are powers not necessarily controlled by either Parliament or the cabinet. In particular it means that the prime minister makes all important military and foreign policy decisions, rather than cabinet. It is true that he may well consult cabinet and allow them to have a full debate, but in the end it is the responsibility of the prime minister to make the final decision. e

In conclusion we can say that the cabinet is still at the centre of the core executive and that most important decisions are made there. The prime minister is its main rival, but ultimately the cabinet can make the most important decision which is to remove the prime minister as happened to Margaret Thatcher in 1990. f

e **17/30 marks awarded.** This answer has a number of good features. It is reasonably well organised and makes a strong case for asserting that the cabinet does remain a powerful body. It shows reasonable understanding of the roles of cabinet and there is some useful evaluation. It does, however, suffer from several weaknesses. It has no real-world examples to use as evidence for its conclusions. It underestimates the extent of prime ministerial control and its argument — that cabinet is still powerful — is not adequately backed up by evidence. a There is a reasonable and clear introduction, although b the statement that cabinet decides in committing troops is dubious. c Descriptions of the cabinet's roles need to be underpinned by examples. d One impressive passage can be seen in paragraph 6, although this point could be better developed. e The prime minister's control over cabinet is described well but this is followed by an assertion that cabinet is central, which seems to contradict what has gone before. f The conclusion is brief and has not been justified by the content of the essay, though the final point is relevant.

e **AO1: 6/10 marks, AO2: 5/10 marks, AO3: 6/10 marks**

Student B

If we travel back several decades and into the nineteenth century we would find that most critics argued that British government was actually cabinet government. Certainly it seems that most domestic policy was determined within cabinet while the prime minister concentrated on foreign policy. In the 1960s, however, critics such as Richard Crossman, a cabinet minister under Harold Wilson, began to suggest that the UK had changed to prime ministerial government. This was the assertion that the prime minister now stood at the centre of the core executive. Furthermore, he or she was able to control the civil service and many of the army of advisers and policy units that now fill Downing Street. The rise of prime ministerial power, of course, suggested the decline of cabinet government. The question we should ask, however, is whether this is still the case. The truth probably is that the dominance of the cabinet or the prime minister depends upon changing circumstances. These circumstances will be examined in this essay. a

There have been some prime ministers who have been very dominant. This was true of Harold Wilson in the 1960s and 1970s when he famously controlled the agenda and meetings of cabinet. He also ruled through an inner cabinet of close colleagues. Margaret Thatcher was perhaps the most dominant prime minister. She used her considerable patronage powers to ensure that the cabinet was filled with her own supporters. She also had very large parliamentary majorities and was supported by a united party for most of the time. She also exercised full control over the rest of the core executive. Decisions tended to be made elsewhere — by Thatcher herself or in cabinet committees — and then she used the cabinet as a rubber stamp for these decisions. b

Tony Blair was also in full control of the cabinet. In fact, under New Labour there was a small group of senior ministers such as Gordon Brown, Peter Mandelson and Robin Cook who made all the key decisions. At least until 2005 the cabinet was totally united behind Blair's leadership and so was not a very significant body. The most dramatic example was when Blair alone took Britain into the invasion of Iraq in 2003. If he had consulted the cabinet the decision may have been different. b

More recently, though, this model of government has become weaker. John Major in the 1990s was unable to control his own cabinet and later Brown and Cameron had to use the cabinet much more extensively. b They did not have dominant majorities and were confronted by powerful adversaries. When Britain had a coalition government in 2010–15 Cameron had to fall back on cabinet government because all decisions had to be made in agreement with two parties. Theresa May must also regularly consult her cabinet because she is involved in such momentous decisions, especially regarding the UK and the EU. She has three ministers — Johnson, Davis and Fox — who are conducting negotiations. c

We do have to remember, however, that although many key decisions are not made in cabinet there are occasions when the cabinet is called on to make key policy decisions. This is especially true when there is a crisis or an emergency. David Cameron had to consult his cabinet as well as Parliament when deciding on military intervention in Libya and Syria. Theresa May will certainly have to consult cabinet in the negotiations with the EU. We also have to remember that the cabinet can remove a prime minister, as it did with Thatcher in 1990. The prime minister can only retain power as long as she or he is able to control cabinet. This means that cabinet is not actually making policy but it does exercise some control over policy. d

The question asks about the cabinet's role in terms of policy making. The answer has to be that most policy is actually made elsewhere in the core executive, especially by the prime minister and her or his key advisers and close ministerial colleagues. This model will vary at different times as this essay has demonstrated and there are occasions when cabinet makes emergency policy but it is more true to say that cabinet has some control over policy without actually making it. e

ⓔ 28/30 marks awarded. This is a strong response which is very focused on the question and makes good use of the facts and arguments in the source. **ⓐ** The introduction is very full and clear and we know how the student is going to organise the answer. **ⓑ** It is especially strong in its use of historical evidence and examples. **ⓒ** There is good evaluation and an excellent review of contemporary realities. **ⓓ** There is also an excellent short but telling piece of analysis. **ⓔ** The conclusion is very strong and comes to a firm conclusion which can be sustained by evidence shown in the body of the essay. There is possibly a slight lack of evidence of cabinet power, reflected in a lost AO1 mark, and possibly a little more evaluation could have been attempted, but these are minor criticisms.

ⓔ AO1: 9/10 marks, AO2: 9/10 marks, AO3: 10/10 marks

Question 2

Using information about at least three holders of the office, evaluate the prime minister's dominance of the political system.

(30 marks)

You must consider this view and the alternative to this view in a balanced way.

ⓔ A useful approach would be to consider first the general knowledge we have about this relationship, showing how *in theory* prime ministers can dominate and also how cabinet and government generally can resist prime ministerial power. Having done this, you should then address the invitation to consider the experience of three prime ministers. Ideally you should choose at least one prime minister who did dominate the political system and at least one prime minister who was less able to dominate.

Student A

I will be using the following three prime ministers to illustrate my answer — Margaret Thatcher, Tony Blair and David Cameron. I will examine the extent to which each of these prime ministers was able to dominate the political system. **ⓐ**

Margaret Thatcher almost completely dominated the politics of her day. This was for a number of reasons. First she won some huge parliamentary majorities of well over one hundred in 1983 and 1987. This meant that she had no problem in getting her policies implemented through parliamentary legislation. She also used her powers of patronage to ensure that the cabinet was filled with her own supporters, such as Willie Whitelaw, Norman Tebbit and Nigel Lawson. She was also able to rid the cabinet of her opponents, whom she called the 'wets'. She was also a very determined character who had a strong political ideology. She was able to impose her neo-liberal and neo-conservative ideas on the political system. Her party was usually united behind her. She also enjoyed the fact that the Labour opposition was very weak because it was divided on left–right wing lines. Finally, we should mention crucial events. The first was the Falklands war, which was a great triumph for her. In addition, the economy, which had been in a bad state in 1979, improved and was very healthy by 1984. **ⓑ**

Turning to Tony Blair there is a similar picture. He won huge parliamentary majorities and led a united New Labour Party. Until the war in Iraq he was also seen as a charismatic and popular figure. He dominated the cabinet through what was known as 'sofa politics'. This meant that he made policy among a small group of his close colleagues. Like Thatcher, most of the cabinet were Blair's allies such as Gordon Brown and Robin Cook. Also like Thatcher, the economy improved under Blair and there was considerable economic growth. One of the other advantages Blair enjoyed was that the Labour Party united around him under the banner of New Labour. **b**

Turning to David Cameron we have a very different picture. He was a much weaker prime minister than the other two described here. Above all he had two problems. One was that he did not win a parliamentary majority in 2010 and so had to govern in coalition with the Liberal Democrats. This meant that he could not dominate the political system. He was also unable to secure a significant majority in 2015. He won a majority of just 12. The other main problem was he faced opposition from within his own party. These were mostly the eurosceptics, who wanted to see the UK leave the EU. This meant that he was forced to order a referendum which of course he lost and was forced out of office. Cameron did have a fairly positive image with the public and the media and the economy was improving but it was not enough to save him from defeat. **b**

So we can see that the prime minister is usually in a very dominant position as long as he or she leads a united party, has a good image and has a large parliamentary majority. However, if he or she lacks these advantages his or her position becomes increasingly precarious. The case studies described clearly indicate this. **c**

e **13/30 marks awarded.** This response has two serious flaws. The first is that although it uses three cases studies and displays a good deal of relevant knowledge it does not widen the perspective to look at the position of prime ministers in general. The second is that it is not evaluative and is one sided in its conclusions. It focuses too much on the powers of the prime minister and too little on the limitations. **a** The introduction clearly demonstrates the limited nature of the approach. **b** The three case studies are conducted reasonably well and are accurate. **c** However, as the limited conclusion shows, the analysis and evaluation in this response are extremely limited and unbalanced.

e **AO1: 5/10 marks, AO2: 4/10 marks, AO3: 4/10 marks**

Student B

There is no doubt that the UK prime minister stands at the centre of the political system. She or he has considerable prerogative powers, is leader of the governing party and controls cabinet government. The prime minister is also the national leader and has a very high public profile. This gives the prime minister great powers. However, there are also limitations on the power of the prime minister and furthermore her or his power will depend very much upon the circumstances of the time. By examining the experience of several recent prime ministers we will be able to critically examine the extent to which she or he can dominate the system. **a**

The prime minister controls the cabinet and Parliament to a great extent. This is because she or he has a mandate to dominate the political system and enjoys the powers of the royal prerogative. She or he is commander-in-chief and conducts negotiations with foreign powers. Above all, however, the prime minister has the power of patronage. This means she or he has the power to appoint and dismiss ministers. Patronage is reinforced by the doctrine of collective ministerial responsibility. The cabinet is under the prime minister's control in that she or he controls the agenda and the membership and work of cabinet committees. **b**

Having said all this, the prime minister is also in the hands of circumstances. If she or he has a very large parliamentary majority, as was the case with Margaret Thatcher and Tony Blair **c** she or he can dominate Parliament. If she or he has a united party which supports her or him, again as happened with Thatcher and Blair, then it is inevitable the prime minister will dominate the system. Both Blair and Thatcher led a government which was packed with their own supporters. We also have to consider the image of the prime minister. Blair, Cameron and Thatcher all enjoyed a positive image, at least until they were discredited — Blair after Iraq, Thatcher over the poll tax and Cameron after the EU referendum. **c**

Prime ministers can certainly dominate the foreign policy agenda. Even Brown, who was an unpopular prime minister, was known for his positive role in dealing with the international financial crisis after 2008. Thatcher was known as the iron lady for her part in the Cold War and Blair was popular abroad for his interventions in Kosovo and Sierra Leone. **c**

Turing to policy, a prime minister with a clear ideological vision can dominate especially if his or her party shares that vision. This was the case with Thatcher (New Right) and Blair (Third Way). John Major led a disunited party (over Europe) and Brown encountered opposition from within Labour, which meant they could not dominate the political agenda. **c**

On the other hand, prime ministers may suffer adverse conditions. David Cameron and John Major both suffered from having small parliamentary majorities or no majority at all. They also encountered a great deal of opposition from within their own party, in both cases over the issue of Europe. This made it difficult for them to dominate cabinet government. In the case of Cameron, of course, he also suffered 5 years of coalition government when he had to negotiate policies with the Liberal Democrats. **d**

Cameron and Brown also shared problems with the economy. Brown was prime minister when a financial crisis occurred, outside his control, and Cameron had to organise a programme of austerity. In both cases this adversely affected their dominance. Image is important too. Brown had a poor public image, as did John Major who was seen as grey and boring. **d**

In conclusion we can clearly see from these examples that there is a mixed picture. Prime ministers have great powers and can dominate but there are also important limitations to their power. However, there are many short-term influences which affect the extent to which they can dominate. The key factors, as shown by the examples, are the size of the parliamentary majority, the state of the governing party, whether there is clear ideological leadership and a host of factors beyond the control of the prime minister, especially international events. e

e **25/30 marks awarded.** Student B has written a strong response with a coherent approach. a The introduction demonstrates that there will be a balance between principles and evidence from the case studies. b The general picture is well described, though this is a slightly limited account. There could be more development of the constitutional and political position of the prime minister. c The evidence from the experience of prime ministers is well organised and is extensive, which is the great strength of this response. d Some evaluation is shown, though again this is slightly limited. The lack of material, for example concerning the fall of various prime ministers, is a problem. e The conclusion reflects accurately the body of the essay and offers a clear summary.

e **AO1: 8/10 marks, AO2: 8/10 marks, AO3: 9/10 marks**

Relationships between the branches
Question 1

Read this original material.

The relationship between government and Parliament

When we think about the relationship between government and Parliament, we automatically tend to think of the House of Commons. This is natural. The Commons is more powerful than the House of Lords and enjoys more democratic legitimacy. But we should also be thinking about the government's relationship to the Lords.

The traditional view of Government–Commons relations is that the former is dominant. This is because the government normally enjoys the support of the majority of MPs and has various ways of controlling how they behave and vote. Of course the extent of executive control does depend on how united the governing party is and on the size of its parliamentary majority. If the government has only a slim majority, as occurred in 2015, a small group of dissident MPs can thwart the will of the government by wiping away the majority. It is really only under such circumstances that the influence of the Commons matches its democratic legitimacy.

The government does not enjoy a majority of support in the Lords. At the same time many peers are extremely independent and do not feel beholden to the party whips. This is largely because, being unelected, they are not accountable. In the 2010–15 coalition government period the Lords was particularly active, especially in such fields as welfare reform and taxation policy.

So we do need to differentiate between the Lords and the Commons when considering this relationship. We can certainly say that, while the authority and influence of the Commons fluctuates depending on short-term political factors, that of the Lords is more constant, that is influential but limited.

Using the source, evaluate the view that the House of Lords is a more effective check on government power than the House of Commons.

(30 marks)

In your response you must:

- *compare the different opinions in the source*
- *consider this view and the alternative to this view in a balanced way*
- *use knowledge and understanding to help you analyse and evaluate*

ⓔ The answer should ideally fall into two parts. The first part might look at the relative powers of the two houses of Parliament, demonstrating the strengths and weaknesses of each. The second part should look at the experience of both houses in recent times. There have been periods when the Commons has looked like the more effective check and periods when the Lords has been more prominent and effective. A firm conclusion needs to be offered, underpinned by relevant evidence.

Student A

There is no doubt that the House of Lords has now become the more effective check on the power of government. This is mainly because of the 1999 reform when most of the hereditary peers were removed, leaving only 92 and the rest appointed peers. It is also because the government does not have a majority in the Lords — far from it — and so cannot guarantee to get any of its legislation passed. There have been recent examples of the House of Lords sending back legislation and threatening to rebel if the government does not change its mind. We also have to remember that many members of the Lords have vast experience — more than many MPs — so they are more able to call government to account and to effectively scrutinise legislation. ⓐ

Many members of the Lords are independent crossbenchers and there are many more Liberal Democrats than in the House of Commons where the party was almost wiped out in 2015. This means that there is a big anti-government majority. In 2017 the Lords forced the government to think again about two amendments to the Brexit bill which they had passed. In the end the Lords lost but it showed the government that it had to think about the issues in the amendments concerning the terms of the UK leaving the EU. Very often it is just the threat of obstruction by the Lords that forces the government to reconsider, as it did about cuts in disability benefits in 2016. These were reversed. ⓑ

There are many members of the House of Lords who have great experience in many fields and so they are well able to prevent the government passing unfair or discriminatory or unclear legislation. Lord Robert Winston, for example, is a great expert on medical matters, while Lord Dannatt is a former military commander and knows a huge amount about military matters. Lord Norton is a politics professor who is an expert on constitutional matters. They make the Lords extremely effective in checking government power effectively. ⓒ

The Lords is still undemocratic but the presence of so many experienced people who are mostly nominated by political leaders, has improved its authority. When it was full of hereditary peers it had little authority and was very limited. This has now changed, though not as much as if it were elected.

There are, however, several limitations to the ability of the Lords to check governmental power. The most important is the Parliament Act of 1949, which says that the Lords cannot veto legislation but can only delay it for one year. It cannot also deal with any financial matters. The Salisbury Convention, which is unwritten, states that the Lords cannot block any government proposals that were contained in the last election manifesto, in other words for which the government has a popular mandate. This does mean that anything not in the manifesto is fair game, but this is unusual. If we add to this the lack of democratic authority enjoyed by the House of Lords we can see that it also has fatal weaknesses. d

The whips in the House of Lords do try to maintain party discipline but this is difficult when there is no majority and so many peers are independent minded. The 'amateur' nature of the House of Lords is both a strength and a weakness. e It is a strength in that it makes peers independent of party control, but it is also a weakness because it means they are neither elected nor accountable.

In conclusion we can say that the House of Lords is now more effective, especially since it was reformed. The House of Commons is largely in the control of the government and its whips whereas the Lords is more independent and is becoming increasingly experienced and professionalised. The balance of power has shifted decisively. f

@ **14/30 marks awarded.** This might be a reasonably strong response if the question were different. Unfortunately, the student has assumed this is an assessment of the power of the Lords. The question actually asks you to compare the Lords with the Commons. Reference to the Commons is very brief in this essay. a The introduction gives a clue to the wrong approach; otherwise it is very clear and useful. The assessment of the Lords is quite strong. There is b c good use of examples and d e good evaluation. Sadly there is virtually no comparison with the House of Commons as is required in the question. There is also virtually no reference to the material in the source. f The conclusion briefly alludes to this, but there is no disguising the fact that this is an unbalanced essay.

@ **AO1: 5/10 marks, AO2: 5/10 marks, AO3: 4/10 marks**

Student B

The source material quite clearly represents the relationship between government and Parliament accurately. For most of the time the government does dominate Parliament although this is not the case when the government lacks a working majority. However, this question is asking whether the House of Lords is more able to check governmental power than the House of Commons. At first sight this appears to be a ridiculous theory because the Commons is the elected house, while the House of Lords lacks any kind of democratic legitimacy. However, there are a number of reasons, both short term and long term, a why it could be said that the Lords has become increasingly effective. This essay will examine the claim that the Lords has indeed become more powerful than the Commons. b

The basis of this claim is that the House of Lords has been reformed and so has become a more professional, active and politically balanced house. The removal of most of the hereditary peers has taken away the inbuilt Conservative majority. Instead there is a balance between peers from the three main parties and a large number of crossbenchers, who are politically neutral. It still does not enjoy democratic legitimacy but it can claim to have increased authority.
c The key point is that the government has no guarantee of getting any of its legislation through the Lords. This was nicely demonstrated in its problems with the Brexit bill in 2017. There have also been problems for the government in the Lords over such issues as disability benefits and educational reform.

The Lords is now full of appointed peers, many of whom have great experience and expertise and so are able to control government even more than many MPs, whose experience of life and work may be more limited. Characters such as Lord Adonis and Lord Sugar are very good examples. This does not mean they will block legislation but it does mean they may effectively amend legislation, sometimes against the wishes of the government.

We do need to be cautious here. There are serious limitations to the authority of the Lords. We have already mentioned its lack of legitimacy, but it is also limited in what it can do by the Parliament Acts (no control over finance and a delaying power lasting only one year) and by the Salisbury Convention, which prevents the Lords challenging the authority of the government's electoral mandate. When it comes to a conflict between the House of Commons and the House of Lords, the government nearly always finds a way of ensuring that the Commons will prevail. Among its methods is the ever-present threat of radical reform (in which case existing peers will lose their places) or even outright abolition.

We do need to ask whether it now has more power and authority than the Commons. **d** The answer must be, as the source suggests, that this depends upon circumstances. When the government has a very large majority and is very united, as occurred under Thatcher and Blair, the House of Commons is very weak. Even a substantial amount of dissent among backbench MPs will have no impact. In these circumstances it may well be that the House of Lords becomes the only effective opposition. This has also occurred since Corbyn became Labour leader. With very little effective official opposition in the Commons, the Lords has felt the need to step in and control the excesses of government. **d**

When the government lacks a large majority or where it is severely divided, the House of Commons suddenly becomes much more influential. The government needs to forge a consensus for all its policies. We saw this under Theresa May, who had a small Commons majority, when groups of dissident MPs caused major problems over the government's proposals for increases in national insurance contributions by the self-employed, the introduction of grammar schools and school funding in general. Despite the weakness of Labour, under May the Commons was undoubtedly more effective than the Lords. In the battle over the Brexit bill in 2017 the Commons certainly prevailed. **d**

In the long term the Commons undoubtedly has more ability to control government power. It has more democratic legitimacy and if it decides to thwart the government there is nothing ministers can do about it. The Lords, on the other hand, lacks democratic authority and there are a number of legal and constitutional limitations that ultimately prevent it from challenging government decisively. However, as we have seen, there are some short-term circumstances when the House of Lords suddenly seems to provide more meaningful opposition than the Commons. e

e 30/30 marks awarded. This is a very strong response worthy of full marks. It focuses on the question, and shows sensitivity to the source, good evaluation, excellent use of concepts such as c legitimacy, mandate and authority and full use of examples to underpin the arguments. a It also shows a very good distinction between long- and short-term factors. This is very often a good approach to questions of this kind on any topic. b The introduction shows clearly the direction of travel of the answer. d There is sensitive evaluation of the differences between the Commons and the Lords as is required by the question. e When we reach the conclusion we are left in no doubt that this is a balanced evaluation but that there is also a firm answer to the question.

e AO1: 10/10 marks, AO2: 10/10 marks, AO3: 10/10 marks

Question 2

Evaluate the ability of the Supreme Court to control the power of UK government. (30 marks)

You must consider this view and the alternative to this view in a balanced way.

e The answer needs to explain the various ways in which the Supreme Court can and does control government power. Having done this an evaluation needs to be undertaken. This should be a balanced analysis with explanations and examples of control and explanations and examples of when government has been able to avoid such controls. The best answers would demonstrate that this is a changing relationship, probably suggesting that the power of the Supreme Court is increasing. Examples of real cases are essential.

Student A

We should first establish the role of the Supreme Court in the UK, which came into existence in 2009 after the Constitutional Reform Act. It is the highest court in the land and the highest appeal court. It deals with interpretations of existing law and also constitutional law. It can also carry out judicial reviews of decisions made by governments at all levels. It also imposes the European Convention on Human Rights (ECHR) when a citizen believes his or her rights have been restricted and it also hears cases of ultra vires when it is claimed that a government body or minister has acted outside their powers. In this way it imposes limits upon government. a

We have to say that these are very wide powers. The most important case in modern history was the Gina Miller case in early 2017. Ms Miller claimed that the government did not have the authority to sign Article 50 taking Britain out of the EU even after the referendum on the issue. Instead, said the court, this can only be done by Parliament. The government was forced to back down and hold a vote in Parliament. So it was that the court had restricted a prerogative power of the government.

The court has also heard cases preventing the government from holding DNA records of people who have not been convicted of a crime, from freezing the assets of terrorist suspects and from holding suspected terrorists for an indefinite period without trial. Of course the court can only impose the laws as they stand. The court cannot make any new laws and this is a limitation on its powers. ⓑ This is the main problem for the court because there may be laws passed which restrict people's rights and there is nothing the Supreme Court can do about it, although citizens can go to the European Court of Human Rights on appeal.

An important factor is that the Supreme Court is now fully independent from government. The independence of the judiciary is established because judges have security of tenure and because they are no longer appointed by politicians. This means that they are very much able to control the power of government because no pressure can be put on them. This means that they can impose the rule of law even if this is inconvenient to the government, especially when it is trying to ensure the security of the state. ⓒ

So, when we consider the Supreme Court's powers we can say that they are extensive and have become greater since the court was made independent and since the passage of the Human Rights Act but that there are limitations to its power because it cannot make laws itself. ⓓ

ⓔ **13/30 marks awarded.** This is a weak answer. In particular, it lacks evaluative and analytical material. It is mostly descriptive. The evaluative elements are extremely brief and limited. ⓐ The introduction correctly describes the role of the court but says nothing about how the answer is going to progress. This is an important omission. ⓑ There is a good passage which describes some key cases but this is not balanced against any weaknesses. ⓒ The material on the independence of the judiciary is relevant, but since the evaluation in this answer is so sparse it is given too much prominence. ⓓ The conclusion does refer to evaluation correctly but this does not reflect what is contained in the essay.

ⓔ **AO1: 5/10 marks, AO2: 4/10 marks, AO3: 4/10 marks**

Student B

Apart from being the highest appeal court and interpreting the law including judicial precedents and case law, the Supreme Court also has a role in controlling the power of government when there is a danger that any of these problems will arise: if citizens' rights are being threatened, if the principle of the rule of law (equality under the law) comes into question and if the government or any other public body is trying to take powers which it does not have under parliamentary statutes. However, the court cannot challenge the government over the laws which Parliament passes. This is because Parliament is sovereign and no court can challenge that. We do not have an entrenched codified constitution in the UK so, unlike in the USA, the Supreme Court cannot challenge any of the laws made by the sovereign parliament on the grounds that they may be unconstitutional. a

There have been many occasions when the courts in the UK have asserted the rights of citizens. In a privacy case called *R* v *Metropolitan Police* in 2011 the court ruled that the police cannot retain the DNA records of people who are not found guilty of any crime. b There was also a case brought by prisoners denied the right to vote and it was claimed this was an abuse of their civil rights. In that case the prisoners won the case even in the European appeal court but Parliament refused to change the law. In 2016 a case was heard concerning the pension rights of men and women and it was ruled that these should be exactly equal. But the most important case was that brought by Gina Miller. She claimed that the prerogative powers of the government did not extend to signing Article 50 — taking the UK out of the EU — unless it received the approval of Parliament. The government, said the court, was trying to exceed its constitutional powers. The government had to give way and a vote was held in Parliament. b

However, there are serious limitations in the powers of the court. Above all other factors is the sovereignty of Parliament. Two cases illustrate the point. The first was the Belmarsh case (heard by the House of Lords but the principle is the same) when nine terrorist suspects claimed they were being held indefinitely without trial, which breaks the principle of habeas corpus. The judges upheld their appeal, but later Parliament simply passed a new law which gave government the power to hold such suspects for 28 days provided a judge approved. It was a partial victory for the court but in the end Parliament had its way. The other case was the freezing of terrorist suspects' bank assets by the Gordon Brown government. Again the court said the government was exceeding its powers, but shortly afterwards Parliament met and gave the same powers to the government. In battles between Parliament and the courts Parliament will always win. b

Nevertheless the Supreme Court has huge moral authority. ⓒ It is definitely politically independent, especially after the Constitutional Reform Act of 2005, which means it stands above politics in its protection of rights and the rule of law if they are threatened by government actions. Even if it can be overruled by Parliament the government knows that if it challenges equality under the law or abuses its authority in some way the rulings of the court may place public opinion against it.

Senior judges often make comments in cases which have influence over Parliament and government. In particular, they will always ensure equality between the sexes and different ethnic groups. The Equality Act of 2010 forbids government or any other body from discriminating on the grounds of sex, disability, age, ethnicity or sexual orientation. The Supreme Court and other courts will always enforce this and the government is aware of it so that modifies their actions. ⓓ

The passage of the Human Rights Act in 1998 was a key development. The Supreme Court now has a set of codified rights which it can use to judge cases fairly, even if government disapproves. This occurred in the Abu Qatada case when the courts refused to allow the extradition of the radical cleric on the grounds that evidence against him was collected under torture. The government and public opinion did not like it but the court wished to impose the right to a fair trial even for an unpopular figure.

In conclusion the Supreme Court is an important protection for citizens against over-mighty government. The lack of a codified constitution and the sovereignty of Parliament do not help its work, but the court, especially the new Supreme Court, does enjoy great moral authority and the judiciary is much more powerful than it has ever been before. ⓔ

ⓔ 28/30 marks awarded. This is a strong response to a relatively difficult question. ⓐ The introduction is very strong, describing the nature of the court and also demonstrating how the answer will progress. ⓑ There is very good use made of relevant cases, showing how they illustrate the power of the courts and the nature of conflict with government. ⓒ It is a very useful idea to introduce the concept of moral authority. This passage also demonstrates sensitivity to the fact that it is not just its judgements that give the court power, but also the threat which it poses to governments which may be considering taking excessive power. ⓓ In general terms there is plenty of evaluation in the answer and the essay is well balanced. ⓔ The conclusion demonstrates this, although there could be slightly more evaluation and analysis, perhaps by referring to the fact that the court cannot initiate action, but can only respond to appeals.

ⓔ AO1: 10/10 marks, AO2: 9/10 marks, AO3: 9/10 marks

Knowledge check answers

1 a Developments establishing key constitutional principles:
- Magna Carta (rule of law)
- Glorious Revolution and Bill of Rights (sovereignty of Parliament)
- Act of Settlement (rules of succession to the monarchy)

b Developments marking significant transfers of power:
- European Communities Act (from the UK to the EU)
- Devolution Acts (from Westminster to Scotland, Wales and Northern Ireland)
- UK leaving the EU (from the EU back to the UK)

c Developments affecting the distribution of sovereignty:
- Glorious Revolution and Bill of Rights (sovereignty moved from the monarch to Parliament)
- European Communities Act (from the UK to the EU
- UK leaving the EU (from the EU back to the UK)

2
- The UK Parliament makes laws.
- The prime minister appoints cabinet members.
- The Supreme Court interprets the meaning of law.
- The Supreme Court and the UK Parliament protect citizens' rights.
- The devolved governments establish regional policies.

3
- Two reforms enhancing human rights are the Human Rights Act and the Freedom of Information Act.
- Devolution has decentralised power.
- Devolution has made the UK more democratic (proportional representation was introduced), as did reform of the House of Lords that removed most hereditary peers.

4
- Three post-2010 reforms that decentralised power were: devolution to city regions; increased powers to the Scottish administration; increased powers transferred to Wales.
- A reform that affects sovereignty is the decision that the UK should leave the EU.
- A reform affecting prime ministerial power is the Fixed Term Parliaments Act, which took away the prime minister's power to establish the date of a general election.

5
- The Scottish government has powers over policing, welfare services, VAT revenue, income tax rates and revenue, air passenger duty and business taxes — all not granted to the Welsh government.
- The Northern Ireland government has control over policing and the law courts, which Wales does not have.

- All devolved governments control education, the healthcare system, transport, agriculture and arts sponsorship.

6
- The Conservatives will probably support the introduction of a British Bill of Rights.
- The Labour Party will probably support reform of the House of Lords.
- The Liberal democrats are likely to support all the reforms except the introduction of a British Bill of Rights.

7
- The prime minister controls foreign policy, alongside the cabinet.
- Parliament and the people control key constitutional changes.
- The health service in Scotland is controlled by the Scottish Executive and Parliament.
- The meaning of the right to a family life is ultimately in the hands of the European Court of Human Rights.
- Whether the government can call an early election is controlled by the UK Parliament.

8 A frontbench MP is either a government minister or officer or a senior spokesperson for a major opposition party, whereas a backbench MP has neither of these positions.

9 The powers held by the House of Commons but not the Lords are:
- scrutiny of the government's financial arrangements
- to veto a bill and so prevent it becoming law
- to dismiss the government through a vote of no confidence

10
- Lord Adonis has expertise in education and transport.
- Lord Winston has expertise in medicine, especially female fertility.
- Lord Dannatt has expertise in military matters.
- Lord Finkelstein has expertise in journalism.
- Baroness Chakrabarti has expertise in human rights and liberties.

11 Debates on the following have been organised by the Backbench Business Committee in recent times. (Other examples can be found on www.parliament.uk/business/committees-a-z/commons-select/backbench-business-committee.)
- Drugs policy in the UK (2014)
- The inquiry into the Iraq war (2015)
- International Women's Day (2015)
- The future of the Post Office (2016)
- Social mobility in the UK (2017)

12 The proposals failed because there was obstruction by the Lords itself. The parties could not agree on what kind of reform to make and there was major opposition from within the Conservative Party.

13 There are many such committees. Prominent examples in December 2016 with the chairperson shown in each case were:
- Economy and Industrial Strategy (Prime minister)
- European Union Exit (Prime minister)
- Parliamentary Business (Leader of the House of Commons)
- Housing (Secretary of state for communities and local government)

14 The poll tax was a proposal to replace the existing form of local taxation, which was known as property rates and was based on the value and size of a person's property, with a largely flat-rate tax levied on each individual irrespective of their income. It was controversial mainly because it took no account of a person's ability to pay and so broke a principle of 'fair taxation'.

15 Collective ministerial responsibility was suspended in 2010–15 because there was a coalition government containing members of two parties. They had to be allowed to disagree publicly because of this. However, collective ministerial responsibility did apply to policies agreed in cabinet between the coalition partners. It was suspended during the referendum campaign because ministers demanded the right to campaign on either side of the issue.

16 The cabinet in July 2017 contained the following: six women; one peer (Baroness Evans); two ethnic minority members (Priti Patel, Sajid Javid). It may have changed since then.

17 The cabinet ministers dismissed in the early days of Theresa May's premiership were:
- George Osborne (Chancellor of the Exchequer)
- Michael Gove (Justice Secretary)
- Nicky Morgan (Education Secretary)
- John Whittingdale (Culture Secretary)
- Oliver Letwin (Cabinet Office Secretary)
- Baroness Stowell (Leader of the House of Lords)

Stephen Crabb (Work and Pensions Secretary) and Theresa Villiers (Northern Ireland Secretary) resigned from cabinet, as did Mark Harper (Chief Whip).

18 Margaret Thatcher's majorities were: 144 in 1983, and 102 in 1987.

19 Tony Blair's majorities were 179 in 1997, 167 in 2001, and 66 in 2005. The dodgy dossier was a report on the reasons why the UK joined the USA in an invasion of Iraq in 2003. It suggested Saddam Hussein, then ruler of Iraq, had 'weapons of mass destruction' and could deploy them at short notice. This was used as the legal basis for the invasion. It was widely believed that the dossier was manipulated to exaggerate the danger and so was 'dodgy'. Blair was implicated in the apparent deception. Thereafter Tony Blair was less trusted than he had been in the past and this adversely affected his premiership and re-election prospects.

20 There are a number of reasons suggested:
- At a time of great economic uncertainty he felt stable government was needed.

- He hoped to extract some concessions from the Conservatives such as House of Lords reform, a referendum on electoral reform and a reduction in taxes for low income groups.
- He hoped to make the Liberal Democrats a credible party of government.

21 The Lord Chief Justice is head of the whole legal system in England and Wales, whereas the President of the Supreme Court is only in charge of his own court.

22 The main Leveson recommendation was the creation of an independent commission to oversee and enforce good conduct of the press in the UK.

23 The Supreme Court ruled there had to be a parliamentary vote to take the UK out of the EU because it would involve changes to the rights of UK citizens. The government does not have a prerogative power to change or remove such rights and so must consult Parliament.

24 *M v Home Office* (1993) was a key case because it established the principle that government ministers could be subject to injunctions to force them to act in a particular way. In other words the monarch cannot be subject to legal proceedings, but ministers can be and are not above the law. This reinforced the principle of the rule of law.

25 *McDonnell v UK* (2014) was a case where the European Court of Human Rights ruled that there had been an undue delay in an inquest in a 'death in custody' case. The court imposed the principle that 'justice delayed is justice denied' so compensation was in order.

26 The last successful vote of no confidence was in 1979. James Callaghan's Labour government had lost its parliamentary majority and was in difficulties with industrial unrest. Parliament decided it was time to call an election (which Labour lost).

27 The House of Lords Act of 1999 removed the voting rights of hundreds of hereditary peers, leaving only 92 able to vote. This meant the House of Lords gained some legitimacy, was mostly made up of life peers and lost its inbuilt Conservative majority which had been provided by the hereditary peers.

28 This was Gordon Brown, who was struggling to deal with a major world financial crisis and dissension against his leadership from within his own party (Labour).

29 There are several possible examples.
- Prominent 'Leave' campaigners include Conservatives Michael Gove, Boris Johnson, Iain Duncan Smith, Liam Fox, David Davis and Andrea Leadsom, and UKIP's Nigel Farage.
- Prominent 'Remain' campaigners include Conservatives David Cameron, William Hague, George Osborne, Philip Hammond and Amber Rudd, plus Nicola Sturgeon (SNP) and Alan Johnson (Labour).

Index